MANAGEMENT BOOKS

General Issues

IN THE PRIMARY CLASSROOM

Pat Hughes

Published by Scholastic
Publications Ltd,
Marlborough House,
Holly Walk,
Leamington Spa,
Warwickshire CV32 4LS

© 1991 Scholastic Publications Ltd

Written by
Pat Hughes
Edited by
Kim Daniel
Sub-edited by
Catherine Baker
Designed by
Joy White
Illustrated by
Jeanette Tunstall

Designed using Aldus Pagemaker

Processed by Pages Bureau,
Leamington Spa

Printed by Richard Clay Ltd

British Library Cataloguing in
Publication Data
Hughes, Pat 1933-
Gender issues in the primary classroom. -
(Management books)
1. Primary schools. Teaching
I. Title II. Series
372.1102
ISBN 0-590-76509-4

Contents

INTRODUCTION

This book is for primary teachers, advisory teachers, headteachers, parents and governors who are interested in gender issues in primary schools. It provides information about what is involved, and gives some simple, practical ideas for the management of equal opportunities.

As adults we are immersed in a lifetime of being male or female. This starts before birth and continues throughout life. One of the first questions asked about a new-born baby is whether it is a boy or girl; in Britain we cannot even name a child until we have this information. It is in fact very difficult to get a greetings card which does not welcome the new baby as either a boy or a girl. It is as if that is the most important thing about this new human being.

Our own immersion in our gender role can blind us to many issues. In order to learn to see, we need to stand back and look again at many of the assumptions we have made, not only about our pupils, but most importantly about ourselves. This may be painful, but it can also be fun.

The questioning process involved is difficult, and for that reason this book provides a more detailed background than would be necessary for many other issues. There is now a great deal of research about gender issues, much of it drawn from the social sciences and the work done by primary teachers in their own schools.

Perhaps the most important recent professional advancement in primary education has been the recognition of the importance of the teacher as researcher. For too long primary teachers have been told what they should or should not do by people whose experience has never extended to a primary classroom. I have spent many years as a teacher of pre-school children, and have also been a class teacher and co-ordinator in a primary school. I have personally tried out many of the ideas in this book, and I have been privileged to know many other primary practitioners who have willingly exchanged examples of good practice.

THE STRUCTURE OF THE BOOK

Chapter 1 provides a background to the issue of equal opportunities. This may be a useful framework for anyone who is having difficulty in persuading colleagues to examine their own practice.

Chapter 2 looks at how gender issues appear within the National Curriculum framework, and the next three chapters look at the management of equal opportunities in relation to each of the core subjects – English, mathematics and science. They examine work done in these areas by professional researchers and by class teachers. Various strategies are suggested to help translate the theory into practice, on the basis of a three-point plan:

• Where are we now?
• Where do we want to be?
• How do we get there?

Chapter 6 looks at equal opportunities management in the foundation subjects, while Chapter 7 examines the whole ethos of the school in relation to equal opportunities, and suggests that more explicit attention be paid to personal and social education in primary schools. The importance of individual teachers in developing the school's ethos is acknowledged, as are the managerial implications for subject co-ordinators as well as equal opportunities co-ordinators. Chapter 8 provides some general advice on the management of equal opportunities at primary school level.

There has been a very real attempt to ensure that the cost of most of the proposals is minimal, since there is little point in making suggestions which require vast amounts of money. For this reason, very little time has been spent on looking at equal opportunities at LEA and central government levels. Whether we like it or not, schools are being encouraged to become more independent, and this will result in the formulation of individual policies and practices which are not LEA-directed.

I am very grateful to the primary headteachers who have shared their expertise in ensuring that governors, parents and the wider community are aware of the implications of their school's approach.

I am also most grateful to all the men and women who have opened my eyes to what must be one of the most fascinating aspects of educational opportunity today.

1 BACKGROUND AND OVERVIEW

EQUALITY

Schools must provide a balanced and broad-based curriculum which:

'(a) promotes the spiritual, moral, cultural, mental and physical development of pupils at school and of society; and
(b) prepares pupils for the opportunities, responsibilities and experiences of adult life.'
(from the 1988 Education Reform Act as quoted in *From Policy to Practice*, DES 1989).

Like most broad-sweeping statements, this sentence begs more questions than it answers. What the Education Reform Act makes abundantly clear is that the National Curriculum is about equality of entitlement. It is about rethinking school approaches to curriculum planning and development.

It would be comforting to imagine that it might be possible for primary schools to achieve this by tinkering around with the existing timetable. However, our knowledge of the educational process has taken us beyond this, and most teachers are conscious of the many other issues which impinge upon them in their role as educators.

The total financial and emotional investment in education is massive. For this reason, the measurement of educational efficiency increases in importance in times of economic constraint. The overwhelming concern with 'value for money' appears at many levels.

Variable factors such as race and ethnicity, economic status, class, special needs and gender produce differences in educational outcomes which are disturbing. For example, black pupils tend to experience different patterns of education from white pupils, and girls tend to have different educational outcomes from boys. The pattern for black girls is different again. These differing educational chances seem to have persisted over time, and the explanations given for them seem to become more complex as we discover more about the educational process.

Until fairly recently, gender issues have been neglected. The present concern about the difference between boys' and girls' outcomes has been highlighted by several government ministers. Their emphasis is almost entirely on the need to ensure that the future labour market is flexible to demand. As Norman Fowler said, when he was Employment Secretary, 'Sex discrimination is not only unfair but harms the economy'. A more liberal perspective might be one of concern over the personal effects of the waste of talent through inequality of opportunity.

One of the major problems in this area has been the difficulty of measuring inequality, particularly at primary school level. Much of the data collected has been in terms of the processes of education involved rather than the more nebulous outcomes, which are only apparent many years after children have left the primary sector.

In order to ensure that the full school experience which children receive is examined, it is important to bear in mind that there are two curricula at work within any school. The formal curriculum is relatively easy to examine. It includes clearly defined teaching subjects, areas of study and structured learning activities. The informal or hidden curriculum consists of much of what is learned at school as an unplanned consequence of the structures and is often, by its very nature, difficult to uncover.

A SHORT HISTORY

'All things bright and beautiful
All creatures great and small
All things wise and wonderful
The Lord God made them all.

The rich man at his castle
The poor man at the gate
God made them high and lowly
And ordered their estate.'

Schooling has been used as a means of 'ordering their estate' ever since compulsory education came into being. In the last century, educators worked to ensure that their charges were equipped to fit the station in life for which they were destined. In the UK this meant that characteristics such as class, race and gender determined the form of education any individual received.

The advent of the National Curriculum has renewed interest in the history of education, in the belief that knowledge of what has gone before can – and should – inform both the present and the future. An examination of the curriculum contained within the different standards set by central government for the schools of the last century can be fascinating. A careful study of the eventual fate of many of the measures designed to influence schooling over the years provides important evidence for anyone who is contemplating the management of change. However attractively the change is presented, the results are rarely as expected.

Another useful function of research into the history of education is to show how aims and objectives for schooling have changed over the years. It now seems incredible that early attempts to educate the masses were greeted with suspicion by many of those with power. It was feared that such attempts would be doomed to failure, or that the masses would get ideas 'above their station'.

The Taunton Commission of 1864 recommended specially designed schools for each social class based on their future occupational roles. Working-class boys were to be trained for their estate in the labour market and working-class girls for theirs in domestic service.

The primary task of the elementary schools was 'the moralization of the factory children through compulsory school attendance; the encouragement of temperance and rational recreation' (Johnson, *Schooling and Capitalism*). Thus the church and state provided schools for working-class boys and girls which ensured that the majority would fit the pattern of the perceived future needs of the labour market. Those who paid taxes which were used to support the schools felt that they had the right, and indeed the duty, to determine what went on in them.

Schooling for girls was seen in relation to a domestic vocation. In the case of working-class girls, this would enable them eventually to provide good homes for their husbands. Prior to marriage many of these girls would be sent into domestic service, working as maids, cooks and cleaners in the homes of the wealthy. Their schooling was seen as a preparation for this type of employment as well as for marriage.

Alongside this gender-differentiated curriculum was the concern that too much education for girls would seriously damage their health and render them unfit for child-bearing. This was based on the belief that the body had only a limited amount of energy and that the demands of childbearing left little for mental exercise. If women over-exercised their brains through too much education, it was felt that they might endanger their ability to produce children.

Meanwhile, a different but related form of education was taking place for the children of gentlefolk. The private and independent schools were required to produce an educated élite who had the necessary skills to rule and govern the country. The sons of the gentry attended these schools, while in the majority of cases their sisters were educated at home. For all sections of society the education of boys and girls was seen as separate, reflecting the widespread belief that education was designed to prepare pupils for their adult life – an adult life which was itself sex segregated.

Class issues have dominated discussion of equal educational opportunity for many years. The 1944 Education Act, which set up a tripartite system of secondary education, was designed to help bright working-class children to fulfil their potential at secondary school level. The failure of the Act to achieve this aim was recognised, and this fuelled the demand for comprehensive secondary education. This programme of educational reform was carried out and supported by the major political parties because it was seen as a means of providing educational equality for pupils, irrespective of their social class. The mixed comprehensive schools were in turn seen as a means of providing a wider curriculum for both boys and girls.

During this process, several studies were carried out to examine children's educational life chances. One longitudinal study published at the beginning of the 1970s identified educational life chances as being related to a variety of factors, including a child's social class, the size of her family, the school's staffing and equipment levels, the parents' educational experiences, the spacing of children in the family, and myopia. It was only later that surveys extended these life chance factors to include race and gender.

Gender issues, then, have been largely neglected until recently. This may in part be because the status of men and women had generally been seen as culturally fixed. Indeed Miss Beale, Headmistress of Cheltenham Ladies College, probably spoke for many when she said in 1865: '[I am looking for] what seems to be the right means of training girls, so that they may best perform that subordinate part in the world to which I believe they have been called'. As recently as 1963, the Newson Report was suggesting that girls should be educated in terms of their main social function – 'which is to make for themselves, their children and their husbands a secure and suitable home and to be mothers'.

THE LEGAL POSITION TODAY

In 1975 the Sex Discrimination Act made it unlawful to discriminate against any person on the grounds of their sex. In relation to education, the Act made it unlawful for a school to discriminate on sex grounds:
• by refusing to admit a pupil;
• in the terms on which it admits a pupil;
• by limiting pupils or refusing to allow them access to any courses, facilities or other benefits of school;
• by subjecting pupils to any other unfavourable treatment.

In the same year, Her Majesty's Inspectorate (HMI) published a survey which examined the extent to which curricular differences and customs contributed to inequality of opportunities for boys and girls. The study included mixed and single-sex schools and involved HMIs covering primary, middle and secondary schools as well as those in further education.

In relation to primary schools, the inspectors found that not only did boys and girls behave differently, but they were expected to do so, and their teachers tended to encourage traditional role-play. The report concluded that there were many subtle differences in the treatment of boys and girls in primary schools which were not desirable. The report indicated that gender discrimination in education often occurred by default rather than by intent.

There has been much discussion over the implications of the Sex Discrimination Act in the education sector, and it has given rise to several court cases, in relation both to pupils and to the employment of teaching staff. There is now considerable case law attached to the Act, which fills in many of the gaps left by the original legislation.

SOME DEFINITIONS

The words 'gender' and 'sex' are frequently used as if they were interchangeable. They are not, and a tighter definition of both terms makes the discussion very much clearer.

Sex differences are biological and invariable; gender differences, however, vary from one culture to another. For example:

Sex difference	Gender difference
• Women can bear children.	• Women generally take on responsibility for childcare.
• A female egg cell contains the X sex-determining chromosome, while male sperm carry the X or Y chromosome.	• The Hausa maintain that 'only women can become ill'.

Sometimes there are obvious discrepancies when biological sex is used as a basis for defining appropriate gender behaviour. For example:

Sex difference	Gender difference
• Women's life expectation is five years longer than men's.	• Many women can retire five years before men and still receive a full state pension.
• Women have a thicker layer of fat under the skin and can resist cold better than men.	• Men are often expected to be gentlemanly and lend coats and jackets 'to the ladies'.

BIOLOGICAL, SOCIAL AND CULTURAL PERSPECTIVES

In the last century, the biological differences between men and women were considered all-important, and the curriculum was designed to give the individual a particular place in the social hierarchy. The curriculum was affected by class as well as gender, but women were seen as intellectually inferior and incapable of sustained study. It was not until the mid-twentieth century, for example, that women were allowed to take a Cambridge degree.

> 'Women are cast in too soft a mould, are made of too fine, too delicate a composure to endure the severity of study, the drudgery of contemplation, the fatigue of profound speculation.'
> (*The British Apollo*, 1708, as quoted in Jan Harding (ed), *Perspectives on Gender and Sciences*.)

This view is rarely expressed so openly today, although dated biological and psychological evidence is occasionally quoted as an explanation for individual differences. The nature/nurture debate has haunted discussions on educational equality, whether it relates to race, gender or class differences. This is essentially an argument about whether it is our biology or the environment within which we grow up that has more important implications for our eventual fate.

Biological determinism has been a powerful way of explaining the observed inequalities of status, wealth and power in society. It also provides a means of defining human 'universals' of behaviour as natural characteristics. When biological determinism is related directly to supposed racial differences its absurdity is particularly striking.

Terman, for example, who introduced the Stanford-Binet IQ test into the US in 1916, wrote that a low level of intelligence

> '...is very common among Spanish-Indian and Mexican families of the South-west and also among negroes. Their dullness seems to be racial, or at least inherent in the family stocks from which they come.... Children of this group should be segregated in special classes. From a eugenic point of view they constitute a grave problem because of their unusually prolific breeding.'
> (Rose et al, *Not in Our Genes*).

Numerous surveys have illustrated the differing child-rearing patterns for boys and girls from the moment they are born. Boys are traditionally dressed in blue, girls in pink. Boys are encouraged to be boisterous, whereas girls are treated with more care. The list is endless, and anyone who has tried to bring up a child in a non-stereotyped way knows how difficult it is to avoid these pressures. The same point is made in the following table, taken from *Untying the Apron Strings* by N. Browne and P. France.

Sex-stereotyped treatment of babies and young children		
Area	**Boys**	**Girls**
Sleeping patterns	Poor sleeping is excused and attributed to liveliness.	Girls need their 'beauty sleep'.
Crying	Not tolerated, therefore dealt with more readily to stop crying. Boys learn to suppress this expression of emotions early on (Belotti 1975).	Babies left to cry. Crying expected from girls and continued to a relatively late age.
Feeding	Given more breast-feed and for longer. Concern if they look underfed.	Given less, weaning earlier. Concern if they look overfed.
Physical play	Rough-and-tumble encouraged between boys and with adults. Assumed to be more active (Loo and Wenar 1971).	Treated with more care. Less adult male play. Assumed to be less active.

Many children come to nursery or school with very clear ideas about what being a boy or a girl means. Girls play with dolls, boys with guns. One of the many tasks of nursery and infant teachers is to ensure that these children's play experiences are extended, rather than restricted to the familiar.

For the purposes of educational equality, the nature/nurture debate is significant if those who believe that behavioural and intellectual differences are biological also believe these differences are inevitable and immutable. *Positive discrimination is needed to help pupils with learning difficulties whether or not these are gender-linked.*

Today

Today's teachers are no longer expected to replicate the previous generation. In fact, they are being positively encouraged to ensure wider educational opportunities for all their pupils. Theirs is the task of educating for an uncertain future. The emphasis on science and technology, problem solving and investigation is a recognition that different concepts, skills and attitudes will be needed in the future.

Different and changing gender roles are certainly part of this. They are among the most delicate of individual rights for, although we are all products of differing socialisation processes, one aspect we have in common is our sexual apartheid. The very term 'opposite sex' implies something different from ourselves. Some grammar books still have lists of opposites, in which man is opposite to woman, as boy is to girl.

For many years secondary teachers voiced concern at the way in which 13-year-old girls and boys selected different subjects when they were making their option choices. Generally, this resulted in boys going for science subjects and girls taking the arts subjects. There was a general feeling that girls particularly were limiting themselves and closing out areas of future employment.

More recently, it has been recognised that boys too face limited and unhappy futures if they restrict their thinking to traditional male patterns. The high rate of suicides among unemployed men is only one result of a society that has kept too rigidly to the view that a man is only worth something if he is engaged in paid employment.

The early studies of gender issues in education were almost entirely secondary-school based. Perhaps this reflected the interests of those engaged with the research, but it also indicates the invisibility of primary education for many of those engaged in other phases of education. In time it became obvious that girls and boys made course and career choices using a wide variety of criteria, many of which were built up during the years prior to secondary education. It became clear that if children's educational opportunities were to be extended in non-sex-stereotyped ways, primary practice would need to be examined.

One of the major purposes of the National Curriculum is to provide entitlement. It will no longer be possible for secondary pupils to 'opt out' of core or foundation subjects at the age of 13. The programmes of study and the attainment targets are designed to ensure uniformity, not just between schools, but also within schools. It is the history of educational reform that urges us to be cautious about the likely result of this. Opting out of a subject can be done mentally as well as physically. Most of us are only too aware of this, when we are faced with some

particularly boring training session. Our bodies may be present, but our minds are far away. Unless pupils actively want to pursue certain subjects, they will 'opt out mentally', and traditional patterns of achievement and failure are likely to persist. These patterns are not just created in secondary schools, although they may be unintentionally reinforced there. Primary schools have responsibilities as well, and one of the purposes of this book is to consider how best to carry them out.

It is important to see the similarities between pupils as well as the differences, and so recognise that learning and teaching may be adversely affected by some gender-related practices. Effective strategies should make life easier for primary teachers and provide plenty of ideas for sound practice.

It is also important to recognise that stereotyping all boys and all girls as representing particular behavioural and intellectual traits is dangerous. All boys are not hooligans, just as all girls are not passive bystanders. Investigating gender issues involves:

• standing back to recognise differences between overall patterns;
• acknowledging individuals in their own right;
• recognising that teachers can influence behaviour.

The wider world

We need to look at the wider world outside educational institutions, because if the gender patterns of the past are to be challenged they also need challenging outside school. Teachers need strategies at their fingertips which they can draw upon to enable their pupils, however young, to challenge traditional and inappropriate sex-role stereotyping. For example, many television advertisements perpetuate a hard macho male image to sell a particular product. If we want to develop responsible citizenship in our pupils, we need to involve them in challenging these images as well as getting them to produce their own criteria for efficient consumership.

Equal opportunities is frequently seen as something for girls and women. The unhealthiness of the Rambo image should make even the most hardened chauvinist hesitate, and question whether we really want our boys to feel that their adult role involves features such as:
- never being allowed to show emotions;
- being tough;
- getting drunk.

Are boys sometimes pushed into dangerous positions because they feel it is unmanly to do otherwise?

Equal opportunities is not about making it acceptable for girls to engage in anti-social behaviour. A taxi driver commented to me, the other day, about the increased number of drunken young women who are involved in fights in his cab. Promoting equality does not involve extending anti-social macho-type behaviour to groups previously unaffected. We should aim to extend the horizons of men and boys as well as women and girls. Males too have much to gain from a wider interpretation of their role. Equal opportunities is about improving the lives of us all.

Other issues

Gender is only one element in our make-up. However, by singling out gender I am focusing on aspects which are often overlooked in the examination of other factors. For example, classroom management problems have often been tackled with no reference to gender issues, although both race and class implications have been examined. Yet, even as far back as the Plowden Report in the 1960s, boys were identified as being more likely to cause disciplinary problems in the classroom, so that at primary level more boys were being seen by educational psychologists than girls. This position was reversed at secondary level, where more girls than boys were referred. Successful strategies for classroom management may therefore need to pay close attention to gender issues, in order to ensure that particular groups of children are not receiving unequal treatment.

At this point it may be useful to establish that we are not trying to search out innate inadequacies (a 'deficit model') of boys or girls. For, as Sheila Lawlor has pointed out very forcibly in her attack on teacher training, the aspiring teacher can be 'trained to imagine that his is a job which, paradoxically, combines a life's work of near unteachable pupils and insoluble problems, and one of inculcating boundless optimism for changing the world and society'. (Lawlor, *Teachers Mistaught*.)

A thorough examination of gender issues is designed to avoid this. For example, one could start by looking at local child-rearing practices. If they appear to be gender differentiated, then we need to examine them, and pull out the features we believe to be the most helpful so that early years teachers can build on their strengths. Close relationships between parents and staff in toddler groups and other pre-school activities can help parents to see the unique individuality of their child as more important than his or her gender. The idea that boys don't cry and girls shouldn't get dirty is easier to confront at a school-based toddler club than it would be if left until the children appear at school for the first time, near their fifth birthday.

In fact, there is considerable evidence that parents do adapt to their own children's individual wishes even when these cross gender lines. The girl who wants a train set for Christmas may get it from parents who recognise her individual wants. On the whole, schools seem to be less tolerant (Newson, 1976).

Cultural practices

The potential conflict between various areas of inequality are frequently glossed over, particularly when considering different cultures. Teachers who are aware of a discrepancy between anti-sexist practices and specific aspects of cultural practices in schools cannot ignore the potential conflict. The resources list at the end of this chapter provides some additional reading on this subject. It would be idle to pretend that this issue can be solved easily. Cultural identity and gender are crucial in an individual's make-up. If we say that we value a multicultural society, we are then in difficulty when we want to question some of the gender-related practices that go on within particular cultures – our own included.

There are practices in all cultures which cannot be condoned, and I think teachers have the right not to feel guilty because they do not embrace all aspects of any particular culture. As teachers, we do have the right to question the cultural practices of our own upbringing and those of others. I was brought up to believe that a good mother did not go out to work. She stayed at home, looked after the house, and made sure that her family was fully prepared for every eventuality. This suited my mother, but both her daughters questioned it and combined parenthood with paid employment. This was frequently accompanied by large doses of guilt, which only eased as the children grew older.

In relation to cultural practices, there are bound to be differences in what is considered acceptable. Personally I cannot accept things such as female circumcision, and denial of access to birth control. A major problem is finding out exactly what is going on in a community to which we have limited access. Frequently we have no idea of what the vast majority of people feel about a certain issue except through the voices of their spokespeople. I am frequently horrified to read in the papers what my own spokespeople say on my behalf.

Any sort of fundamentalism is dangerous, for it denies the rights of individuals to information as well as to decision-making. Equality is about duties and rights as well as about choices. This is what we must work towards.

IN-SERVICE STRATEGIES

Discussing our own educational experiences

Our own educational experiences affect how we see ourselves as teachers, and indeed as human beings, and how we feel about gender, race and class.

One way of examining this issue is to ask staff to discuss in pairs how they became primary teachers in the first place. This can raise some interesting points about the differing careers advice and support given to young men and women. The following quote from a female primary teacher on an in-service course illustrates this well.

'In my grammar school, the A stream went to university, the B stream trained as teachers and the C stream became secretaries and nurses. We didn't need careers advice; we knew what we had to do'.

Nature/nurture – What is natural? What is normal?

The purpose of this exercise is to raise issues about how the word 'natural' is used. Sometimes it is used to mean that people behave in a particular way because they are biologically programmed to do so. Sometimes it simply means 'normal'. Normality can be measured in a statistical sense. Few women are over six feet tall, but some are. 'Natural' has several meanings.

Write up the following statements, and ask colleagues to discuss the different points raised by each one.

1. It is not natural for women to carry heavy loads.

2. It is not natural for women to be over six feet tall.

3. It is not natural for a man to want to stay at home and bring up his children.

4. People from the professional classes are naturally better parents than others.

5. People from some races are naturally more intelligent than others.

6. It is natural to want to go home at the end of a hard day at work.

7. It is not natural for boys to play with dolls.

8. It is not natural for girls to play with train sets.

A historical perspective

The following three extracts provide a background to the changing perspectives on women's education. There are plenty of statements similar to the first two to be found in literature, and often in the daily papers. One way of opening up a discussion on this issue is to give your colleagues all three extracts, but without their sources and dates, and ask them when they think the pieces were written.

'The whole education of women ought to be relative to men. To please them, to be useful to them, to make themselves loved and honoured by them, to educate them when young, to care for them when grown, to counsel them, to console them and to make life sweet and agreeable to them – these are the duties of women at all times and what should be taught them from their infancy.'
(Rousseau, *Emile*, 1762.)

'One always rather likes the Nigger, evidently a poor blockhead with good dispositions, with affections, attachments – with a turn for Nigger Melodies and the like: he is the only Savage of all the coloured races that doesn't die out on sight of the White Man: but can actually live beside him, and work and increase and be merry. The Almighty Maker has appointed him to be a Servant.'
(Thomas Carlyle, 1867.)

'• The principle that each pupil should have a broad and balanced curriculum which is also relevant to his or her particular needs is now established in law.
• That curriculum must promote development in all the main areas of learning and experience which are widely accepted as important.
• The curriculum must also serve to develop the pupil as an individual, as a member of society and as a future adult member of the community with a range of personal and social opportunities and responsibilities.'
(NCC, *From Policy to Practice*, DES 1989, 2.2.)

Canvassing opinion

This exercise is most effective when several schools are working together on an in-service programme designed to raise awareness of the issues involved in equal opportunities. It provides a fairly safe method of gathering people's views and then working together on what to do next. You need at least twenty people taking part in the workshop.

Give each member of the group a piece of paper with the 'opinion finder' on it (see page 22). One of the four questions should be circled on each copy, and each participant should canvass opinion on his or her circled question before proceeding to Stage 2.

OPINION FINDER

Since there are likely to be differences of opinion between individuals about the questions below, it is suggested that you start with one-to-one interviewing of at least three people if possible. Try to find people you don't know well, or whom you don't see often.

Stage 1

• Make a note of the opinion and the reasons for it.

• Don't worry about who said what – this session is intended to canvass ideas which will be recorded at the next stage, but which do not have to be defended.

Questions

1. In what ways might equal opportunities be significant for you in your work role?
2. In what ways might equal opportunities be regarded by different members of your school?
3. In what ways might equal opportunities be regarded by the members of the wider school community?
4. How would you like your school to be perceived in terms of equal opportunities?

Stage 2

Now join up with the other people who have the same question ringed on their sheet, in order to report back all the opinions expressed.

• *First* give your own opinion on the question.

• *Next* give the opinions you heard from other people.

• *Finally* record all the opinions on one sheet of paper and select one person to report back to the whole group.

Stage 3

Feedback and forward planning.

Support from outside

Many new ideas can best be introduced by someone from elsewhere – for example, an advisory teacher, a university lecturer, or a teacher from another authority – who can come in, provide training to a particular brief and then walk out again. They are often able to describe what is happening elsewhere, and can raise the issue away from the personalities within a small primary staffroom. They may also be in a position to offer support and resources to a school which is just starting to explore gender issues.

RESOURCES

Government publications

Department of Education and Science (1987) *The National Curriculum: A Consultation Document* (DES/WO).

Equal Opportunities Commission (1976) *A Guide to the Sex Discrimination Act* (EOC).

EOC (undated) *Do You Provide Equal Educational Opportunities?* (EOC).

EOC (1985) *Equal Opportunities and the School Governor* (EOC).

National Curriculum Council (1989) *From Policy to Practice* (DES).

General

Browne, N. and France, P. (1986) *Untying the Apron Strings: Anti-sexist provision for the under-fives* (Open University Press).

Johnson R. (1976) 'Notes on the schooling of the English Working Class 1780-1850' in Dale, R. England, G. and MacDonald, M. (Eds) *Schooling and Capitalism* (Routledge & Kegan Paul).

Newson, J. and Newson, E. (1976) *Seven Year Olds in the Home Environment* (Macmillan).

Lawlor, S. (1990) *Teachers Mistaught* (Centre for Policy Studies).

Rose, S. Lewontin, R. C.and Kamin, L. (1984) *Not in our Genes* (Pelican).

Race and Gender

Davies, A. (1982) *Women, race and class* (Women's Press).

Hooks, B. (1981) *Ain't I a woman: black women and feminism* (Pluto).

Fuller, M. (1984) *Inequality: Gender, Race and Class* (The Open University, E205, Block 6, Gender, Race and Education).

Kamm, J. (1958) *How Different from Us: a biography of Miss Buss and Miss Beale* (Bodley Head).

Taylor, H. (1984) 'Sexism and racism: partners in oppression' in *Multicultural Teaching* vol 2(2).

Taylor, H. (1984) 'An open cupboard policy' in *Issues in Race and Education*, 41.

Troyna, B. and Carrington, B. (1987) 'Antisexist/antiracist education – a false dilemma: a reply to Walkling and Brannigan'; in *Journal of Moral Education*, 16, 1.

Useful Addresses

Advisory Centre for Education (ACE)
18 Victoria Park Square,
London E2 9PB.

Department of Education and Science
Elizabeth House,
York Road,
London SE1 7PH.

Equal Opportunities Commission:
England
Overseas House,
Quay Street,
Manchester M3 3HN.

Wales
Caerwys House,
Windsor Lane,
Cardiff CF1 1LB.

Scotland
St Andrew House,
141 West Nile Street,
Glasgow G1 2RN.

Northern Ireland
Chamber of Commerce House,
22 Great Victoria Street,
Belfast BT2 2BA.

National Foundation for Educational Research in England and Wales,
The Mere,
Upton Park,
Slough,
Bucks SL1 2DQ.

National Curriculum Council
15-17 New Street,
York YO1 2RA.

Scottish Education Department
New St Andrew's House,
St James' Centre,
Edinburgh EH1 3SY.

Welsh Office
Education Department,
Crown Buildings,
Cathays Park,
Cardiff CF1 3NQ.

2 GENDER ISSUES AND THE NATIONAL CURRICULUM

OFFICIAL PUBLICATIONS

The red consultative document on the National Curriculum which appeared in July 1987 made little mention of equal opportunities. There were other areas of schooling which it also failed to spell out in much detail, notably multicultural education, careers guidance, health education, citizenship and economic and industrial awareness. The document saw schooling in traditional terms, as subject matter waiting to be delivered to an eager and homogeneous mass of pupils. Initial reactions to the document were based on the belief that schooling and education amounted to very much more than this. Various school-based activities were identified as cross-curricular and not limited to one particular subject discipline. Primary experts, in particular, questioned the philosophy of what appeared to be a very secondary-orientated subject timetable.

One result of this concern was the establishment of the National Curriculum Interim Whole Curriculum Committee under the chairmanship of Malcolm Brigg. Later publications from the NCC set out in greater detail what was meant by the term 'cross-curricular issues'.

The first of the NCC series Curriculum Guidance came out in 1989. Entitled *A Framework for the Primary Curriculum*, it examined several issues:

'• planning the curriculum;
• continuity within the curriculum;
• implementing the curriculum;
• the education of children under five'.
(1.3)

It stated that the planning of the framework should:

'• be flexible enough to allow for a range of approaches to the planning of the whole curriculum and the organisation of learning and teaching in primary schools;

• ensure a whole-school approach to implementing the National Curriculum;
• recognise the entitlement of all pupils to a broad curriculum as embodied in the core and other foundation subjects: this being regardless of race, gender, disability or geographical location;
• improve communication between schools, governors, parents and LEAs;
• inform all aspects of planning and efficient use of resources both human and material;
• ensure that the monitoring of pupils' progress takes place, together with consistent, informative record-keeping'.
(1.4)

The guidelines included a step-by-step approach to curriculum planning from a whole-school perspective (2.7), suggesting that the basic subjects should be set in the context of the whole curriculum of the school by examining current policies or initiating new policies to include:
• multicultural education;
• equal opportunities;
• personal and social education;
• special educational needs;
• information technology.

'These dimensions should be woven throughout the life and work of the school, in every area of the curriculum, and be addressed by every teacher. It is essential that there is a common school viewpoint which will guarantee a consistent approach'.
(2.7iii)

Circular Number 6, *The National Curriculum and Whole Curriculum Planning: Preliminary Guidance*, was distributed to schools in December 1989. It pointed out that the basic curriculum as prescribed in law (i.e. the ten core and foundation subjects of the National Curriculum plus religious education) was not intended to be the whole curriculum. The circular hoped to offer some preliminary help in planning a whole-curriculum framework and to identify some issues which schools needed to consider when setting the National Curriculum in a broader context.
It reiterated the Education Reform Act's statements that the curriculum should:

• be balanced and broadly based;
• promote the spiritual, moral, cultural, mental and physical development of pupils at the school and of society;
• prepare pupils for the opportunities, responsibilities and experiences of adult life.

The circular then suggested that, in order to achieve these aims, schools needed to ensure that the planned contribution of different subjects was not made in isolation but 'in the light of their contribution to pupils' learning as a whole'. Three aspects of cross-curricular provision were identified and examined in much greater detail than before: cross-curricular dimensions, skills and themes.

Cross-curricular dimensions

These were seen as concerned with the 'intentional promotion of personal and social development' through the curriculum as a whole. It was recognised that this personal and social development could not be left to chance, but needed to be co-ordinated as an explicit part of a school's whole-curriculum policy.

Equal opportunities and education for life in a multicultural society were identified as major cross-curricular dimensions. These need not necessarily entail a course of personal and social education (PSE), but they were considered necessary to promote personal and social development. They required 'the development of positive attitudes in all staff and pupils towards cultural diversity, gender equality and people with disabilities'.

Cross-curricular skills

Oracy, literacy and numeracy skills were identified as cross-curricular; they could be developed through all subjects.

Cross-curricular themes

These were seen as elements that enriched the educational experience of pupils. They included:
• economic and industrial understanding;
• careers education and guidance;
• environmental education;
• health education;
• citizenship.

In May 1990, Number 3 of the Curriculum Guidance series (*The Whole Curriculum*) was published. This document examined these elements in relation to the curriculum as a whole. It further defined what was meant by a cross-curricular dimension (page 2). Dimensions were to be seen as a commitment to providing equal opportunities for all pupils and a recognition that preparation for life in a multicultural society was relevant to all pupils. Equal opportunities 'is about helping all children to fulfil their potential'. The document recognised that teachers were right to be concerned when their pupils underachieved, and to be aware that educational outcomes could be influenced by factors outside the school's control such as sex or social, cultural or linguistic background.

It was acknowledged that entitlement to the curriculum involved access and that there were often subtle barriers which stood in the way of such access. Cross-curricular dimensions were expected to permeate the whole curriculum, and be woven into the life of the school. It was no longer enough to have a policy statement. Curriculum guidelines in all subject areas needed to take account of these cross-curricular dimensions and any curriculum audit should see them as an essential part of the school ethos.

These recommendations reinforced the idea that the National Curriculum is about entitlement, and provided useful criteria to enable schools to examine how far individual children receive this entitlement.

Part Two of *The Whole Curriculum* examined the practical considerations involved in whole-curriculum planning under three headings:

• curriculum audit;
• whole-curriculum development plans;
• implementing whole-curriculum development plans.

Curriculum audit involves matching existing provision against the curriculum requirements of the Education Reform Act, and helping to prepare a whole-curriculum development plan. The audit covers both curriculum review and evaluation. A checklist for curriculum review was provided in *The Whole Curriculum*, which suggested that an analysis of the curriculum could be aided by using a range of prompts and questions. For cross-curricular elements the following prompts were suggested:

'Where do cross-curricular dimensions, skills and themes appear in the curriculum? Where are the gaps? Where is there duplication? Is a co-ordinated approach used? Where does specific responsibility for cross-curricular elements lie? Are the essentials embodied within subjects or timetabled separately?'

Further questions were suggested as part of the school's own evaluation procedures, such as, 'How far have objectives been met? What have been the successes and failures and why?'

More generally, the curriculum audit should involve schools in examining their own policy documents in relation to certain issues. The matters under consideration should include the consistency of the documents with national and local guidelines, their reflection of the needs of the school and its pupils, and their status as working documents.

Once a school has completed its curriculum review and evaluation, whole-curriculum development plans can be drawn up. Again the guidance document pointed out that these would be in the form of working documents, subject to constant updating. A separate heading, 'Managing Curriculum Change', considered how cross-curricular dimensions could be implemented. It recommended that during *any* policy review a school should ask itself whether it had policies for particular aspects of the curriculum such as equal opportunities and multicultural education.

MONITORING THE NATIONAL CURRICULUM

School-based monitoring

Curriculum development plans are one method of monitoring and evaluating how the process of National Curriculum implementation and development is progressing. This is initially done at school level, but monitoring is also the responsibility of the Local Education Authority and Her Majesty's Inspectorate.

LEA monitoring

Many LEAs have produced a standardised format for formulating a School Development Plan (SDP). The monitoring of race, gender and special needs issues within this plan will vary from one LEA to another. So too will the criteria on which the reviews and inspections carried out by

LEA officers are based. The Standard Assessment Tasks (SATs) and Teacher Assessment will provide additional data for evaluation.

HMI monitoring

By the middle of 1990, HMI had already carried out two surveys on how a selection of primary schools were managing the National Curriculum. At this early stage, it was rather like planting potatoes on Good Friday and digging them up on Easter Sunday to see how they were getting on. Certainly the reports could do little more than examine the organisation and delivery of the three core subjects.

More useful in relation to equal opportunities are the sorts of comments to be found in the HMI school inspection reports. These are freely available from the Department of Education and Science, Publications Despatch Centre, Honeypot Lane, Stanmore, Middlesex HA7 1AZ. They give some idea of the sort of things that HMI are looking for:

'At the time of the inspection most schools were reviewing their schemes of work to improve the quality of the curricular planning. Their existing guidelines do not sufficiently inform lesson planning, nor do they offer guidance on equal education opportunity for boys and girls, for ethnic minorities or for children with special needs. Pupils' work is regularly assessed and parents are informed of their children's progress. Most schools invite parents to help with aspects of the work and arrange meetings for parents to learn about school policies and activities. These arrangements encourage positive links between home and school.'

'Approximately two-thirds of the staff hold incentive allowances above the main professional grade. These are mainly associated with the weight of duties undertaken. It is noteworthy, however, that only 30 per cent of women compared with 64 per cent of men held posts at grade B or above; the imbalance is even more marked in the higher grades and above.'

'The general commitment given by the teachers to equal opportunities for girls and boys does not yet have a consistent effect on the work of the school. On the contrary, in some lessons boys take the bulk of the teacher's attention. The teachers need to devise practical strategies in order to implement the school's policy on equal opportunities.'

The views of HMI in relation to gender issues are also contained within the series *Curriculum Matters*. For example, *History from 5 to 16* recommends that when planning a history course one should '... pay greater attention than was formerly the case to the position of minority groups and the role of women in history'.

Information Technology from 5 to 16 notes that 'for various reasons the interest that boys have in technical artefacts is frequently reinforced during the late primary years and adolescence, whereas that of girls often lacks encouragement'.

Later, specific strategies are offered to rectify this, such as counselling and computer clubs.

DEFINING EQUAL OPPORTUNITIES

One thing which the NCC has failed to clarify is exactly what it means by the term 'equal opportunities'. Several of the local education authorities have been more forthright, as indicated by their job advertisements.

Advertisements like these cover a multitude of different categories. At the minimum they provide a statement about being an equal opportunity employer, or striving towards being one. At the other extreme there is an attempt to ensure that every imaginable category is covered.

Schools, however, need to develop their own meanings for the catch-all phrase 'equal opportunities'. Those primary schools which have already engaged in equal opportunities policy-making are likely to be aware of the dangers of too narrow a definition, for it may often exclude more than it includes. Too wide and bland a definition is equally unhelpful, as it prevents specific monitoring and target-setting. Policy-making at this level quickly becomes meaningless, useless and time-consuming, which is dispiriting for everyone concerned.

MOVING TOWARDS EQUAL OUTCOMES

A useful image employed some time ago by the Manpower Services Commission, when training secondary teachers, was that of a series of stages. The Commission was keen to widen the option choices made by boys and girls in secondary schools. They analysed the existing equal opportunities policies of schools in terms of four images – the unlocked door, the open door, the special escalator, and equal outcomes.

• The *unlocked door* is the situation when there is nothing to stop pupils undertaking an activity. In the secondary sector this would mean that boys wanting to study home economics would not be prevented from doing so. In a nursery class, it might mean that construction equipment is set out and that there is no reason why any pupil should not use it. In both cases, certain groups have been failing to open the door and make use of the educational opportunities provided for them.

• The *open door* moves on from this to provide some form of encouragement for pupils to undertake activities that they seem to be avoiding – for example, actively encouraging girls to take physics in the secondary sector and in the primary sector encouraging boys to play in the home corner. Again, the policy met with a discouraging response from some groups.

• The *special escalator* policy acknowledges that there may be informal barriers to equality which need to be broken down. A special computer class for girls might help them to become more familiar with the technology involved, by providing them with experiences in school which they may not be getting outside school. The aim of the class would be to make them less likely to give up on information technology. Another, more common example of this approach is where additional help is given to those children who are having difficulties in a particular area of the curriculum, for example with reading.

• The final stage offers all pupils *equal educational outcomes*. As the DES document *From Policy to Practice* states:

'The principle that each pupil should have a broad and balanced curriculum which is also relevant to his or her particular needs is now established in law.

'That principle must be reflected in the curriculum of every pupil. It is not enough for such a curriculum to be offered by the school; it must be fully taken up by each individual student.'
(2.2)

STRATEGIES FOR DEFINING EQUAL OPPORTUNITIES

Establishing ownership of change

All those who have been involved in the management of change, either as the agents or as the subjects of change, will recognise the importance of believing that the change has something to offer them. The technical term is 'ownership of change'. For those involved, it provides a feeling that their views and opinions have been valued, and that the change will be of benefit to them.

At school level, the starting point for any issue is to review what colleagues consider the terms involved to mean. This can be carried out formally or informally, but some form of consensus needs to be reached.

Defining equal opportunities

A redefinition of equal opportunities, for present purposes, could be 'equal *education* opportunities'. This has the advantage of limiting strategies to those which are achievable within the primary school.

Developing the idea of equal opportunities for boys and girls

Equal opportunities needs to be seen as concerned with boys and girls, men and women. It is about developing potential, and should be seen as an essential part of good practice. It is not about boys being made into girls, or girls becoming boys. It is about extending the educational life chances of all pupils, irrespective of race, gender or special needs.

Gender-linked problems in society

At the moment, gender-linked problems exist in our society for which schools must hold some responsibility.
• Many girls fail to think further than becoming wives and/or mothers. This limits their career potential, as they make option and career choices for the short term.
• There is evidence that many boys choose options and jobs which provide a high pay level, but give little personal job satisfaction.

• Many women are financially dependent on their partners or on the state. Those who work in paid employment tend to be in the traditional sectors of female employment, where pay scales are low. Even those who are in equal-pay jobs, like teaching, still find themselves at the lower end of the pay scales.

Earnings: Great Britain 1987	
Average gross hourly earnings, excluding the effects of overtime, of full-time employees on adult rates:	
	pence per hour
Women	386.2
Men	526.2
Differential	140.0
Women's earnings as a percentage of men's	73.4

(Source: *Department of Employment Gazette*)

• Many working women operate a 'double shift'. This involves taking on the sole or main responsibility for domestic work and childcare as well as paid employment.
• Many men miss out on the parenting of their own children; equally, children, whether in two-parent or one-parent families, frequently miss out on being parented by their fathers. This occurs for several reasons. Babies tend to arrive at a point in men's careers when time taken out would have severe repercussions. Also, society still sees childcare and domestic work as female activities, and it is difficult for men to move against the subtle pressure to conform. The gradual increase in career-break schemes for women and childcare facilities at their place of work is not being replicated for men. Furthermore, because of an increase in the divorce rate more men are now separated from their children.
• Many men find it difficult to combine the macho stereotype with forming caring and mutually supportive relationships with their partners, children or friends.
• Sexual harassment ranging from wolf-whistles to rape are a daily reality for girls and women.
• Violence, including football hooliganism, vandalism and bullying, is a predominantly male activity. This has brought about a prison system which is almost entirely

devoted to the containment of men, which raises questions about why it is that more boys than girls are failing to learn what schools teach about acceptable ways to behave.

• Special needs pupils tend to be boys. The Fish Report (1985) on special needs showed that 86.6 per cent of the pupils in schools for children with emotionally disturbed behaviour are boys. In areas where there are many pupils from ethnic minorities, a disproportionate number of black working-class boys are likely to be considered to have special educational needs. Boys are generally referred twice as often as girls for treatment of speech problems, hearing, visual and other physical disabilities, and emotional disturbances. In some special schools and classes, the pupils are likely to be almost all boys. It is reasonable to question whether gender issues are involved in the identification of children with special needs. The key question here is whether there are genuine differences in the levels of attainment, or is it that boys are generally more difficult in class and, therefore, more likely to be labelled as having special educational needs? Once labelled, they are more likely to be removed from the class. Girls who may need help can be overlooked if they are quiet and acquiescent.

Whole-school planning

It is important that a curriculum audit for any subject area considers cross-curricular issues such as equal opportunities. In a primary school this means that all staff have to be involved in ensuring that NC recommendations are incorporated into their curriculum planning. Even in schools which have someone specifically designated as an equal opportunities co-ordinator, each subject co-ordinator will still need to make sure that his or her own policy statements have a strong cross-curricular dimension.

The hidden curriculum

Strategies need to be developed for monitoring the informal or hidden curriculum of the school. These will need to include the identification of the various elements which make up the ethos of the school.

Developing knowledge

Teachers and pupils require an understanding of gender issues in order to help them put aside the influence of traditions, customs and prejudices.

EQUAL OPPORTUNITIES POLICY MAKING

The curriculum guidelines set out in *The Whole Curriculum* assume that most schools already have a policy for equal opportunities. However, many schools have deliberately waited before committing themselves to written policy statements, while some existing policy statements are of very little value. Successful statements on equal opportunities will usually include the following items.

• A clear statement about equality of opportunity for all, regardless of sex, race, class or disability (a few schools also include sexuality, trade union activity and religion).

• Identification of areas of concern and good practice. Every school is unique, and its policies will reflect this.

• Consideration of school organisation, classroom practice, curriculum, resources and adult role models.

A first step towards a school policy may be to monitor existing practice. Schools and the individuals who work in them start from different points; genuine change in attitudes, values and practices takes time.

School organisation

Children are still sometimes segregated by sex, with separate lines, separate registers, separate cloakrooms and different jobs. These give official approval to differences between the sexes, and contribute to children's self-image as well as the skills they learn. Good practice needs to be identified and pursued throughout the school.

Resources

• Books and other learning materials need to be monitored to ensure that they are non-sexist and non-racist. You can use checklists like those shown opposite to help with this.

• Existing materials should be examined carefully and stereotyped images avoided.

• Positive images of both sexes should be promoted.

• Use of resources such as playground space, computers, science and maths equipment should be monitored and allocated fairly.

NB Few books can be expected to meet all the criteria mentioned in the first checklist opposite, but such lists can help ensure that a wide selection of books in school present children with positive images of themselves and others.

The second chart opposite is adapted from Steve Harrison and Ken Theaker's book *Curriculum Leadership and Co-ordination in the Primary School* (Guild House Press, 1989).

Checklist for reading materials

Book title	Women/ girls excluded or omitted	Men/ boys excluded or omitted	Men/boys in stereotyped roles or activities	Women/ girls in stereotyped roles or activities	Presence of people from a variety of backgrounds	Presence of people with special needs	Inclusive language

Selection of non-book materials

1. Presentation	stimulating	attractive	unattractive	
2. Purpose	display	occasional handling	regular handling	
3. Size	appropriate	inappropriate for intended age/stage		
4. Construction	robust	adequate	flimsy	safe/ unsafe
5. Durability	good	average	poor	
6. Date of production:				
7. Suitable for ages:				
8. Unit cost £... Relative cost	high	average	low	
9. Usage by	individuals	pairs	small groups	
10. Appropriate for specific curriculum areas:				
11.Equal opportunity principles	good	poor	none	
12. Cultural diversity	good	poor	none	
13. Replacement cost	high	medium	low	
14. Refill availability	good	poor	none	
15. Storage needs – secure?	yes/no			
16. Teacher guidance notes	good	poor	none	

Classroom practice

• Constant use of words such as 'he', 'man', and so on excludes women and girls and should be avoided by both staff and children.
• The attention given to pupils should be fairly divided.
• Organisation of resources and activities should ensure equal use and participation by all pupils, including children with special needs.

Curriculum

• All children should have equal access to all aspects of the curriculum.
• Bias in subjects should be identified and eliminated.
• Children should be encouraged to understand the nature of prejudice and discrimination. The issue of gender equality can be discussed with pupils of all ages.
• Assessment procedures need monitoring to ensure that they are not distorted by stereotyped attitudes and expectations.

Adult role models

• Schools should provide opportunities for pupils to see women and men in a wide variety of work and home roles.
• All those coming into the school need to be made aware of the school's policy.

Staff development

Policy making should involve all those who work in a school. The school's staff development policy should:
• allow staff to participate in training opportunities;
• ensure that staff are aware of their responsibilities in implementing policy;
• ensure that all staff are valued, supported and encouraged.

The starting point for good practice in equal opportunities will vary from school to school. Policy making needs to reflect this, and should be continuous. Attainable targets should be set, and constant monitoring and updating should be undertaken in order to ensure progress.

It is worth remembering that genuine change is a slow process, and that the area of gender issues is a particularly delicate one, since it involves personal opinions as well as professional judgement. A good equal opportunities policy is simply a guide to good educational practice.

Several LEAs have produced guidelines and policy statements to help primary schools. Leeds LEA, in its document *Equal Opportunities Guidelines for Primary Schools*, takes the three National Curriculum dimensions of race, gender, and special needs and provides three separate programmes covering equality in each area, none of which contains unnecessary verbiage. The additional black and white photographs of children provide examples of good practice. Photographs are one excellent way of remind us all that equality is about children and that it involves the celebration of our many differences as well as the humanity which we share.

Policy statements need to be adapted to the particular needs of any one school. This checklist shows the way in which one primary school made such an adaptation:

St Gabriel's School Checklist

1. Realise that you as the teacher are a role model and focus of attention for the children and that staff attitudes are fundamental in any attempt to counter sex stereotypes.
2. We will never divide children into boys and girls.
3. Train girls to lift and carry, boys to tidy up and help smaller children.
4. Ensure that wherever possible resources and materials are non-sexist, and prepare our own non-sexist materials.
5. Encourage children to explore new roles and activities.
6. Introduce new toys in a non-stereotyped way.
7. Girls and boys will be involved in all curriculum aspects, whether it be crafts, sports, science or technology.
8. Teach about changing sex-roles in theme work, history and drama.
9. Encourage mathematical confidence through the solving of practical and mechanical problems.
10. Encourage non-stereotyped social behaviour.
11. Observe classroom interactions with the help of a colleague.
12. Show that we approve of girls and boys playing together.
13. Invite male/female visitors in non-traditional occupations/roles.
14. Replace competition with co-operation.
15. Remember that teaching staff are primary teachers, not always Infant or always Junior teachers.

The checklist shows very clearly the priorities of this particular church school, and reflects the many different contributions of members of staff within the school. Like many checklists which have been formed by working teachers, it is not a tidy document. In fact, the copy I was given had several additional comments written on it. The school's staff see their work in the area of equal opportunities as ongoing, and predict that this checklist may be developed to become more encompassing. Its current importance is to act as a focus for staff discussions about equal opportunities practice within the school.

EQUAL RIGHTS

In time, the staff of any school may find that it is useful to draw up something approaching a general equal rights policy. This would have the advantage of emphasising the basic needs which we all share, whatever our race and regardless of gender. The term 'special needs' takes on a much wider and perhaps more useful meaning in this context, since we are all special, and we all have particular responsibilities as well as rights.

Lynn Davies, Director of the School of Education International Unit, University of Birmingham, has suggested the following 'Bill of Rights':

'1.A right to dignity and respect, and a responsibility to accord dignity and respect to others.
2.A right to recognition, and a responsibility to give recognition to others.
3.A right to an environment free from bias or discrimination, and a responsibility to create that environment for others.
4.A right to an awareness that one's own culture is changeable, and a responsibility to try to understand and evaluate others' cultures.
5.A right to personal growth in terms of a range of skills, and a responsibility to help the growth of others.
6.A right to satisfaction and sense of achievement, and a responsibility not to allow this satisfaction to be bought at the expense of others' sense of underachievement.
7.A right to fun, stimulation, interest and laughs, and a responsibility not to deny this to others.
8.A right to participation in decision-making, and a responsibility for the decisions that are made.'
(Davies, 1990)

A similar approach has come from the Anti-racist Teacher Education Network (ARTEN) in the form of 19 recommended criteria for a 'Curriculum for Equality'. These criteria emphasise the need for teachers to intervene in the implementation of the National Curriculum and to transform it to ensure that 'good education' operates to provide a 'full range of life chances for as many students as possible'.

Both the ARTEN criteria and the Bill of Rights offer various ways in which the National Curriculum cross-curricular dimensions could be interpreted, but on the whole the former are very much more radical than the latter.

The development of separate policy statements for each of the cross-curricular dimensions may be a necessary first step to an overall equal rights policy for the school, as this would enable all members of staff to look more closely at the effects of current unwritten practice. The very process of writing a policy statement involves the raising of awareness, even if only in the mind of the writer. Ideally, of course, all policy statements should be drawn up by the whole staff. It would after all be particularly ironical if a policy document on equality were foisted upon an unwilling staff!

RESOURCES

Government publications

Department of Education and Science (1987) *The National Curriculum: A Consultation Document* (DES).

DES (1989) *National Curriculum: from Policy to Practice* (DES).

Her Majesty's Inspectorate (1988) *History from 5 to 16*, Curriculum Matters 11 (HMSO).

HMI (1989) *Technology from 5 to 16*, Curriculum Matters 15 (HMSO).

HMI (1990) *The Implementation of the National Curriculum in Primary Schools: A survey of 100 schools* (HMSO).

National Curriculum Council (1989) *A Framework for the National Curriculum* (NCC).

NCC (1989) *Circular 6: The National Curriculum and Whole Curriculum Planning: Preliminary Guidance* (NCC).

NCC (1990) *Curriculum Guidance 3: The Whole Curriculum* (NCC).

Curriculum co-ordination

Harrison S. and Theaker, K. (1989) *Curriculum Leadership and Co-ordination in the Primary School* (Guild House Press).

General

Brooking, C. Foster, M. and Smith, S. (1987) *Teaching for Equality: Educational resources on race and gender* (Runnymede Trust).

Davies, L. (1990) *Equity and Efficiency? School Management in an International Context* (Falmer Press).

Fish, J. (1985) *Educational Opportunities for all: Report of a committee reviewing provision to meet special educational needs* (ILEA).

3 ENGLISH

ENGLISH AS A CONTROVERSIAL ISSUE

'Man interposes a network of words between the world and himself, and thereby becomes the master of the world'.
(Georges Gusdorf, quoted by Bullock, 1975.)

Controversy is never far away when English is discussed, and since all primary teachers teach English, they too are involved in many of the dilemmas inherent in language teaching. The examination of gender issues within this already difficult area has particular problems. For this reason, there follows a short explanation about why the teaching of English creates so much disagreement and why the raising of gender issues in relation to language is often met with misunderstanding.

Even the title given to this core subject, 'English', has been seen as a retrograde step by some primary specialists. 'Language' is all-encompassing, but 'English' is perceived more narrowly as a subject discipline. Language has been likened to gravity – one of those things with which everyone is familiar, but which few people can adequately explain.

One basic tension which makes English such a controversial subject lies in the fact that language is both personal and social.

Language as our personal property

As the quotation from Gusdorf at the beginning of the chapter implies, language is the vehicle of our internal thoughts. The mastery of language, therefore, is an important part of our personal and social identity. Our personal language reflects our individual experiences; it becomes our individual property. Since our gender is also part of this personal and social identity, gender issues are inextricably woven into the way we choose to use language.

Language as community property

Language is also social. It provides the all-important communication between individuals. The differing gender identities within society ensure that gender is also relevant to language as a communal property. For language is the means through which ideas, perception and concepts are transmitted between individuals. Primary pupils learn how others communicate, the linguistic rules they obey, the style they use, the symbols they employ to describe the world and to order their knowledge of it. The language environment in which pupils operate therefore influences not only how they communicate but also how they conceptualise and think about the messages to which they are exposed.

Comb your hair, Jane, you look like a gypsy.

Can't you talk properly?

Now sit down quietly and no talking!

I'd like two strong boys to move this box

Did I ask you to talk?

Teachers as language guardians

Not only do teachers have to help children's cognitive development through their language skills, but the wider social role of language also brings with it obligations. There is the belief that someone or some body should be responsible for the maintenance and upkeep of language, that a series of rules and regulations should guide and structure our verbal communications system.

Teachers are considered an essential part of the process of preserving this communal property. Children need to be taught the words and structures of language, and they inherit the task of passing them on to the next generation. The duty to preserve language is given extreme importance by people who feel that those who break the language rules are guilty of polluting the common resource.

The attempt to question language in terms of its classist, racist and sexist assumptions is seen by some as part of the pollution of language, and as something to be resisted *per se*. This is the argument of the status quo, which fails to see language as a living entity. If our thinking is to be flexible for an unknown future, our language should reflect this.

Primary teachers as communication facilitators

Linked to the guardianship of language is a further requirement. The National Curriculum documents on English have shown that an essential role of the primary teacher is to teach skills, attitudes and knowledge about language. It is not enough to allow it to develop spontaneously. Some of the most bitter discussion about particular aspects of language teaching, such as beginning reading, are disagreements about the level of support needed. That primary teachers should be seen as key personnel in transmitting information about language is obvious. It is exactly how the teacher does this that has become one of the most important discussion points in the debate about language teaching in the primary school.

Language reports

Primary teachers, whether they like it or not, are caught up in the conflict between language as a personal possession and language as community property. This conflict was reflected in the reports published prior to the publication of the Final Orders: the Kingman and Cox Reports.

These reports aimed to explore English teaching in schools. The Cox Reports were followed up by a huge consultation process involving teachers all over Britain.

One issue taken up by the reports is the never-ending debate on the relative importance of register in English. This in turn links with the question of educational opportunities in relation to social disadvantage. The Cox Reports (see below) examine this in detail, yet the Final Orders for English do not contribute to the debate. What is worrying is that the discussion (which has been part of the process of the Final Orders) may be lost over time. This loss would result in a failure to mark many of the equality issues involved in the use of language, of which register is just one example. Strategies which examine gender in language and language teaching form an essential part of developing pupils' knowledge about language.

The Kingman Report

The Kingman Committee was set up to investigate HMI's suggestion that children, and their teachers, needed to 'know about language'. The implication behind this was that knowledge about language was a means of improving standards. This directly acknowledged belief in a series of structures and words which need preserving as part of our communal heritage.

An analysis of the model of language outlined by the Kingman Report provides useful perspectives on gender issues, although these were not explored in detail in the Report. The model was in four parts:

• The forms of the English language – sounds, letters, words, sentences – and how these relate to meaning.

• Communication and comprehension – how speakers and writers communicate and how listeners and readers understand them.

• Acquisition and development – how a child acquires and develops language.

• Historical and geographical variation – how language changes over time, and how languages which spread over territories differentiate into dialects or indeed into separate languages.

There are gender issues involved in how we communicate with others, and how we acquire our understanding of what other people mean when they communicate with us. Our acquisition and development of language is largely social and, if our gender identity plays a part in our social development, it is likely to inform our language development too.

It is also possible to argue that knowledge about language must involve knowledge about gender structures within language. Research into language and gender has enjoyed a phenomenal growth in the last ten years. Only a limited amount of this can be reported here, but more detailed accounts are mentioned in the Resources section on page 69. Several of the practical strategies suggested have used ideas from this research to provide an informed theoretical framework compatible with National Curriculum requirements.

The Cox Reports

The importance of children having knowledge about language was taken up again by both Cox Reports, and was reflected to a lesser extent in the Final Orders. The Kingman and Cox Committees assigned an important role to literature, and the Cox Reports even listed recommended authors. Their overall criteria for choosing books involved an acknowledgement that bias and stereotyping should be confronted. But certainly not all the works of the named authors are themselves free of bias and stereotyping.

The Cox Reports recognise the mutually supportive nature of the elements of reading, writing, talking and listening, but again the longer discussion which was available for readers of these reports could not be carried on into the Final Orders. Much of the background information from the reports will therefore need to be reflected in the in-service brief of the language co-ordinator.

The language co-ordinator also has the task of ensuring that the cross-curricular dimensions of race, gender and special needs will permeate the school language programme. The non-statutory guidelines note this obligation, but provide little practical support (B1). The pervasiveness of English throughout the curriculum means that the language co-ordinator's role is particularly wide, affecting resources in all curriculum areas. One advantage of drawing up criteria for purchasing resources – see the charts on page 39 – is that other co-ordinators can check that newly purchased materials fit the agreed criteria.

ENGLISH AND GENDER ISSUES

At this point gender issues will be examined in relation to English. In order to provide a sound framework for discussion, the evidence about performance and attitude differences will be examined first, and then the biological, social and cultural perspectives which may be involved. This provides a good starting point for examining the curriculum content before moving on to the implications of all this for primary pupils and their teachers.

Performance and attitude differences

Until we start to get data from the Standard Assessment Tasks (SATs), most of the hard evidence about differences in performance between boys and girls comes from the secondary level. Examination performance at O and A Level indicates that not only do more girls than boys take examinations in English, but also a higher percentage of those taking the examinations pass.

School examinations: England and Wales 1986-87		
	Boys (thousands)	**Girls (thousands)**
Attempted CSE/O Level English Language	321.9	328.9

GCE A Level English	Boys (thousands)	Girls (thousands)
Attempts	12.9	29.7
Passes	10.5	24.4

Standard Assessment Tasks will provide data to show whether these overall differences at 16 and 18 are reflected at earlier ages. Certainly in the days of the 11-plus, girls scored considerably higher than boys on the English papers, and several published tests used standardisation methods which required girls to achieve a higher score than boys in order to pass. Some schools are still using these very dated tests.

The discussion over SATs has mostly concentrated on the differences they are likely to reveal between schools in relation to special needs. It is also likely that over the years they will provide evidence of differences concerning those two other cross-curricular dimensions – race and gender. Already schools with a higher than average intake of 'disadvantaged children' have expressed concern at the proposed publication of results. If gender-related differences are found in English scores at seven and eleven, the sex composition of any school is likely to become an important issue as far as their published results are concerned.

A further cause for anxiety is that performance indicators in English teaching in primary schools remain elusive and vague. The continuing controversy about the teaching of reading indicates the particular problems faced when attempting to measure performance using different data. Assessment for the National Curriculum attainment targets and statements of attainment for English requires a much more detailed and standardised breakdown of performance and, as with all record keeping and assessment under the National Curriculum, it entails 'monitoring the performance of constituent groups such as boys and girls, and members of ethnic minorities' (NCC *Curriculum Guidance* 1, 3.3 iv, 1989).

In the past there has been a surprising lack of research into gender differences in English regarding performance and attitude. Class-related differences in language have been studied much more, and have produced a great deal of intellectually stimulating and controversial literature as well as several school-based projects. These have examined and tried to influence what goes on before school entry as well as afterwards.

Reading

It is not easy to find recent data from primary schools in relation to gender differences in reading. During the 1978 DES Primary Survey HMI found that boys obtained a lower mean reading score when tested at nine, and that this difference was statistically relevant. However, children tested in reading at eleven did not show significant gender differences. Both sets of data indicate that boys' scores tended to be at the extreme ends of the distribution curve. The primary language surveys carried out by the Assessment of Performance Unit (APU) found that, on average, girls learn to read more quickly than boys, and that they prefer to read fiction, while boys prefer information books.

Recent documentation from HMI does not comment on gender differences in performance, although 'opportunity classes and remedial reading sessions tend to be dominated by boys'. Work on reading scores, such as the controversial leaked report in July 1990 from a group of psychologists concerned about the drop in reading standards, has failed to make any mention of differences between boys and girls.

Speaking and Listening

'If the women in your street tend to yak over the garden hedge, do what they do in Meikleour, Perthshire – grow big hedges. The Meikleour beech hedge has a trimmed height of 85 ft. Mind you, it was planted in 1746, so you may have to wait a bit for some peace and quiet.'
(*The Pint Size Guinness Book of Records*, no. 4: *High Society*, quoted in Graddol and Swann, 1989)

Folklore has it that verbal ability is an area of feminine expertise, particularly in the years before school begins. Maccoby and Jacklin, researching into gender differences in the 1970s, found evidence to show that girls do speak sooner than boys, and use longer sentences earlier. However, this early start on the part of women does not necessarily prevent men from having more than their fair share of time when it comes to conversation in adult life!

The one area that is reasonably easy to study is that of grammar acquisition, and there is evidence to show that girls, as a group, use a greater variety and greater number of words, whereas boys have a wider vocabulary in particular areas of interest.

The National Curriculum English documents have highlighted the importance of speaking and listening. Research at adult and secondary level has shown that men and boys have significantly different speech patterns from women and girls. In mixed groups, women ask far more questions than men and interrupt less. They use more minimal responses such as 'mm-mm' and 'yes', which seem to act as support mechanisms for conversation. Most surprisingly to some people, men talk more than women. In single-sex groups, women hesitate less and elaborate more, whereas men tend to argue more and negotiate for status.

The monitoring of verbal classroom interaction at both secondary and junior school level has tended to replicate these finds. In secondary schools, boys get in some cases as much as 60 or 70 per cent of the teacher's time. At a recent literacy conference in Manchester, a primary teacher described how she had monitored group talking using topic discussion cards on moral issues. She found that in single-sex groups girls were more task specific and goal orientated, that they supported each other more in conversation and responded verbally to the verbal contributions of other girls. In the boys' single-sex groups, individual boys seemed to have more difficulty in contributing to the verbal contributions of other boys in the group, and they tended to compete with each other for verbal time.

Several teachers working through action-based research within their own primary classrooms have found that particular pupils, usually boys, have developed distinctive verbal strategies which were particularly effective in gaining the teachers' and fellow pupils' attention. Shouting out, interrupting other speakers and providing unusual answers are techniques used frequently by some pupils to ensure that they receive more than their share of teacher attention.

A study carried out in six Cleveland nurseries by a seconded nursery teacher found that the number of adult/child exchanges were approximately the same for each sex, but that the nature of the exchanges was different.

This table is taken from Julia Hodgeon's report for Cleveland LEA and the EOC, *A Woman's World?*

Adult-initiated adult-child interchanges		
Type of interchange	Adult/girl	Adult/boy	Adult/mixed group
1. Offers help	62%	35%	3%
2. Questions intention	55%	33%	12%
3. Social interaction: non-play	58%	31%	11%
4. Elaborates play	34%	46%	20%
5. Offers information, description	30%	43%	27%
6. Questions for information, description	39%	40%	21%
7. Directs/manages	36%	46%	18%
TOTAL	42%	41%	17%

No longitudinal surveys have examined gender issues involved in learning to speak and listen in school, so we cannot tell how strategies develop over time. It is tempting to suspect that the gender-differentiated attitudes found in the nursery are replicated throughout schooling. Monitoring classroom interaction is one way for an individual teacher to find out whether children are being treated differently on the basis of their gender.

The evidence to date indicates that there are important gender differences in adults and children's speech patterns, and that these become more obvious over the years at school. In class, some speech patterns may help to gain additional time from the teacher, but they may also be inhibiting learning. If talk is important for learning, then girls are getting less opportunity to express themselves, develop concepts, question and explore ideas through talking. Also, girls' education and upbringing may be giving them less chance to acquire and practise certain registers, such as those associated with competitive public debate. At the same time, boys may also be developing a competitive attitude towards talk, rather than a co-operative one.

Poor listeners may be missing much that is transmitted orally, and they may also be failing to learn important social conversational skills. If boys are more likely to be in this category, they will also be failing to develop a good overall strategy for adulthood.

Teachers can use simple charts like the one opposite to help them assess the gender implications of classroom interaction. It is impossible to record everything that is going on in a classroom, and so checklists such as the one on page 55 concentrate on a limited selection of teacher and pupil behaviours.

Writing

Gender analysis of written work has shown that girls are more likely to write descriptively, whereas boys tend to use words which are more precise in their meanings.

One of the problems of this type of evidence is that the findings tend to be highly subjective. One report about creativity, sex-role socialisation and pupil-teacher interaction at pre-school and primary school level in Australia found that teachers were more likely to see boys at the most creative and least creative extremes. The report also found that boys received more encouragement because teachers saw them as being more creative.

More systematic data collection has since become available. At secondary level, the National Association for the Teaching of English (NATE) Language and Gender Committee examined English GCSE coursework. They were concerned that girls' and boys' selections were unnecessarily restricted. They did not see either boys' or girls' choices as inherently better or worse; rather they wished to see a 'balanced diet' of subject matter for both sexes.

In primary schools the APU primary language surveys found that many girls said they enjoyed extended creative poetry and letter writing, and they could see a wide variety of purposes for writing skills. Girls on the whole tended to enjoy writing about their families and their personal experiences. Boys, however, said that they preferred to be given factual episodic writing assignments, and they could see far fewer purposes for writing skills than the girls could.

Equal opportunities checklist for verbal classroom interaction

Number of boys:

Number of girls:

Activity/lesson taking place:

Time	Teacher asks question		Pupil answers		Pupil asks for help		Teacher gives help		Teacher reprimands pupil		Pupil comments spontaneously	
	Boy	Girl	Boy	Girl	Boy	Girl	Boy	Girl	Boy	Girl	Boy	Girl

The National Writing Project produced a theme pack on issues related to gender and writing. In this, they highlighted two areas of concern:
• that the range of activities and topics selected by boys and girls is unnecessarily restricted;
• that the material children read promotes gender stereotyping which is reproduced in their own writing.

The pack then goes on to investigate strategies to extend pupils' writing in non-stereotyped ways.

BIOLOGICAL, SOCIAL AND CULTURAL PERSPECTIVES

The literature is silent on possible biological differences between boys and girls in relation to language development. However, there is some evidence about the social and cultural perspectives in primary language teaching, which may form part of the subtle process of social conditioning.

Even before starting school, gender-differentiated child-rearing practices may have influenced children's language development. There is evidence that girls spend more time indoors than boys, and this may involve them in more practice at oral communication. This could help explain the apparent verbal superiority of pre-school girls.

Once in school, other factors operate. That old chestnut, teacher expectations, may have an effect on performance; indeed, several studies have indicated that it does. Unfortunately such research is seldom well-documented and the teachers concerned are often asked impossible questions. One study compared five infant teachers who believed that boys were almost as good as girls at learning to read with five teachers who believed that boys were not as good as girls. All the children involved had similar reading scores and came from similar backgrounds. After a while, according to the researchers, the boys taught by teachers who believed they were almost as good as the girls were progressing as well with their reading as the girls, whereas the reverse was true with the other group. No mention is made of all the other factors involved, or of the likely effect of outside researchers coming in to monitor one particular aspect of reading.

More useful was some work done in four Hull primary schools in the 1970s. Here the researcher monitored the language used in school, and found that children were being exposed to language which was gender-differentiated. She found that many of the adjectives teachers used when rewarding or punishing pupils had sex-related qualities. Naughty boys were 'boisterous, rough, aggressive, adventurous'. Naughty girls were 'fussy, bitchy, giggly and catty'. The latter terms are far more derogatory than the adjectives applied to the boys.

Controversial words

The Equal Opportunities Commission pamphlet, *An Equal Start*, gives a selection of adjectives and asks teachers to put them in columns according to whether they think the words apply to girls, boys or either. Older primary pupils have little difficulty in doing this. The following words are included in the exercise:

gentle	sissy	brutal
boisterous	bossy	sensitive
kind	cheeky	cute
rough	strong	aggressive
pretty	babyish	timid
competitive	competent	spiteful
dependent	helpful	clinging
warm	energetic	emotional

The Commission asks teachers to consider why some adjectives seem so closely related to sex, and whether these terms really apply to all the children they know.

Generic terms

If you want to start an argument, one of the easiest ways is to bring up the question of the use of 'man' as a generic term. It is certainly a tidier term than 's/he', and it avoids the use of still-unfamiliar neutral terms such as 'chair' and 'fire officer'. It does mean, however, that children have to learn it as a generic term, and this may exclude women from many of their visual images.

There is a certain amount of evidence for this, which teachers can replicate in their own classrooms. Young children can be asked to respond to descriptions involving the generic term 'man'. They tend to do this by drawing males. Once the definition is specifically widened to include women, girls and women appear in the drawings.

The language of assemblies provides some of the most obvious examples, with phrases such as ' the Family of Man' and 'all men are Jesus' brothers'. Teachers can focus on the concepts their pupils are making from these words.

CURRICULUM CONTENT

The first and most important 'textbook' a child in the UK is likely to be given in primary school is one from the school reading scheme. Even in schools where no reading scheme is used, books are used to teach reading in a way that does not happen again as children grow older.

For many years there was little discussion about the content of reading scheme books. The important aspect was the method of teaching involved.

Over the past twenty years, however, the content of the books presented to young children has been examined at length. The Bullock Committee on Literacy in 1975 found that not enough attention had been given to book content and its effect on children's attitudes. They suggested that 'any reading scheme should stand up to questions about parental roles, sex roles, attitudes to authority etc.' They also stated that children's reading experience should not be confined to a 'restricted range of reading matter presenting a narrow range of attitudes'.

The non-statutory guidance provided for teachers in the English National Curriculum document reminds schools of the need to review teaching materials so that they comply with 'policy on equal opportunities.'

Most primary schools have now taken this often repeated message on board. Certainly, most publishing companies have had to adapt in order to ensure that their reading material fulfils the criteria which good school language policies suggest. Initially, concern concentrated on the 'detached house' phenomenon, where all the people lived a particular style of life. This resulted in a broadening out of the visual experiences offered in the books, rapidly followed by an awareness that cultural and sex stereotyping were also important matters for consideration. Today, almost all reading schemes do try to address issues of race and gender.

The prohibitive cost of completely updating the book stock in any school has meant that many primary schools still use books which portray the old racist, sexist and classist images. This is a matter of concern, as there is considerable evidencethat the behaviour of children does vary after listening to and reading sexist and non-sexist books and stories. In studies of nursery-school children, the children increased the number and type of jobs they thought were appropriate for women after hearing stories featuring working mothers. A documented study of seven- and eight-year-old pupils found that when female main characters were presented in active roles, pupils were more likely to believe that both boys and girls could succeed in doing the activities featured in the stories.

Many pupils are aware of the misrepresentation of their own experiences in what they read. There are several important teaching points about book content which even very young children can be encouraged to consider. It is particularly important to make children aware of the issue of stereotyping in books if they have to use old and outdated materials because of a lack of resources within their school.

STRATEGIES: WHERE ARE WE NOW?

Existing policy

Examine the existing English policy document to ensure that the school's policy on equal opportunities is reflected in its language policy.

Resources

Examine all the resources within the school. Older pupils can be used to help with this, and the checklist for reading materials on page 39 can be modified for their use. Staff who are hesitant about the feasibility of examining resources might note the following HMI comments about the resources, displays and library in one primary school:

> 'Although a start has been made, the base-line is low. There are some multicultural resources including jigsaws, dolls, pictures and books, but these are offset by some displays which do not present positive images of various races, for example a Third World display in the junior hall, and the existence of some books in the infant library which are racially stereotyped.'

Monitoring classroom interaction

This is difficult, but it can be done in a variety of ways. It is unrealistic to expect that primary schools will be able to afford additional trained staff to monitor classroom interaction. Therefore teachers need to develop their own evaluation skills. Some of the suggestions made in the section on speaking and listening (see pages 63 and 64) could be adapted so that tasks set as a regular part of programmes of study incorporate rather than 'add on' monitoring perspectives.

The Schools Examination and Assessment Council publications on detailed assessment in primary classrooms made this type of monitoring look unnecessarily difficult. If taken in gradual stages, in teachers' own time, it can be far more fruitful, less threatening and even fun.

Step 1: taping a lesson or activity

This is an excellent reminder of who does the most talking and what they talk about. Nobody else need ever hear the tape, and it can provide useful pointers as to where most of your attention goes. I have found taping groups of children very much harder, unless I am actually sitting with them and can note down who is talking. I found this impossible as a class teacher, so I limited the taping to whole-class activities and discussions. When other adults are present, taping small groups is easier, provided you make sure the adults understand what you are trying to do.

Step 2: monitoring individual children

Record how individual children spend a particular day. Start with just two children and note down every 20 to 30 minutes what they are doing. When I did this recently, I was horrified to discover that one child, a girl, whom I had noted as a quiet, careful worker, was not in fact speaking to anyone at all during the observation time.

Step 3: detailed classroom observation

Behaviour

The use of simple checklists can help you identify task-related patterns.

Verbal exchanges

Detailed verbal exchanges between pupils, and between pupil and teacher, are very much harder to monitor systematically. Whole-class discussions are one way of starting the monitoring process, and most primary teachers are already aware of the friendship patterns of the children in their class. It is important to take care to identify and note the very quiet children as well as the more vociferous ones.

Reading and writing

Noting who makes most use of any areas of the classroom set aside for reading and writing can reveal gender differences. There may also be observable differences in attitudes to tasks involving reading and/or writing. Older children can monitor their own reading patterns and be provided with opportunities to reflect on what they have read. Many teachers already do this, and will only need to note if there are any gender implications.

Monitoring classroom management

Discuss with colleagues the classroom management strategies needed to cope with children who demand much more time than others. Less experienced teachers, particularly, need more help and support in this area than established practitioners often realise.

Monitoring language in school

Genderwatch! (SCDC, 1978) suggests a series of questions related to the language ethos of the school.

Spoken language – staff

• How are staff addressed by colleagues – Mr, Mrs, Miss, Ms, Nora, Linda, Mike?
• How are pupils expected to address staff – Mr, Sir, Madam?
• If the form of address indicates marital status for some staff but not others, does it matter?
• Who addresses whom by first name and why?
• Are there any roles in the school which, because of the language used, are assumed to be occupied by women or men only, for example 'dinner ladies'?
• Is use made of gender-specific terms – for example headmaster, headmistress? What gender-neutral items could be used to replace them?
• Is the male or female pronoun generally used to refer to any of the people listed in staff handbooks and booklets about the work of the school?

Spoken language – pupils

• Does the school have a disciplinary procedure for the use of sexist and racist terms of abuse – between pupils or between staff and pupils?
• Are male and female pupils referred to differently – for example, girls by first name and boys by surname?

Printed and written language

• How are pupils listed in the school's registers and records? Is there a justification for listing female and male pupils separately?

• How are letters or other communications to parents and guardians addressed – for example, do they assume that all the children have two parents?

• Does the Prospectus reflect, in language and images, the proportion of females and males in the school, both pupils and staff?

• Are the images and language used in videos, films and slides monitored for sexist and racist assumptions?

• Are textbooks and worksheets monitored for racist and sex-stereotyped assumptions in their use of language and images?

• What policies could be adopted for using current stock and for future buying?

• Do communications cover the languages spoken and read at home?

WHERE DO WE WANT TO BE, AND HOW DO WE GET THERE?

The answers to the question 'where do we want to be?' might well include the following:

• In a school where language is used to develop the potential of all those who work within its walls.

• In a position to be able to identify strategies already in use for monitoring and assessing children's performance.

• In a school where identifiable short-term and long-term targets have been agreed by staff.

• In a school where there is an awareness of, if not a commitment to examine, the wider issues involved in language teaching.

There are various ways in which these and similar aims could be met. The following ideas might be a start:

• Develop a language policy which recognises the existence of gender differences in language acquisition, and provides a framework for boys and girls to acquire a full range of language skills.

• Provide practical examples of how pupils can examine and look at these issues.

Different strategies will be needed by different teachers in different circumstances. The ideas that follow have been used by teachers with some degree of success. The Resources section at the end of this chapter lists some publications which tackle similar issues.

Speaking and listening

Clear objectives

Class and group discussions need to be managed carefully. It helps to have a clear idea of the purpose of the discussion. Class discussions may have different aims, such as:
• to share information and ideas before starting a piece of individual or group work.
• to feed back from an individual or group activity;
• to look at a particular issue, such as fights at playtime;
• to make a decision – for example, what to do about playtime problems;
• to plan how to do something – for example, a display on the wall.

Interruptions

Older children can monitor interruptions themselves. One teacher chose two nine-year-old pupils to do this for her using a clipboard. Verbal and non-verbal interruptions were noted and afterwards discussed with the whole class. Teaching points were made about the importance of listening skills, and a series of strategies were used to develop these skills. The idea that listening skills are about good manners, as well as about helping us to learn, comes in as part of any personal and social education (PSE) programme.

Conversational skills

Conversational skills can be developed in pupils who may have very real difficulties for a variety of reasons. In this case, teachers have to build up good relationships with children who need to trust before they commit themselves to speech. Developing conversational skills also involves:
• valuing, and teaching pupils to value, the languages of children whose first language is not English;
• valuing, and teaching pupils to value, the efforts of those who have special needs in communicating.

Skills of affirmation, listening and co-operation

Several different projects have examined ways to build up skills of affirmation, listening and co-operation. It is useful to introduce these slowly with the whole class, so that children can transfer the skills they have learned to their work in small groups.

Three useful examples are listed below, but there are now several books and resource packs available which can provide many more (see Resources, pages 69 to 70).

• Listening for a minute. Ask the children to close their eyes, sit in silence for a minute, and listen to the sounds inside and outside the room. Then they should say or write what they have heard.

• Magic shell or microphone. Only the child with the magic shell or microphone is allowed to speak. After speaking, she or he passes it to the next speaker.

• Story telling. One child starts to speak, holding a microphone, and after a minute passes it on to someone else, who has to continue the story.

The National Curriculum documents provide many additional ideas for developing oracy, and the National Oracy Project has advised teachers to be aware of gender perspectives. It is this awareness as well as the specific ideas for oracy that will inform good practice.

There is also real concern that if performance in speaking is assessed by asking questions and making statements, this may be discriminatory for girls and quieter boys. Many classrooms are still expected to be fairly quiet and when girls keep to this rule they may be judged badly for it.

Reading

Analysing materials

It is fairly easy to join with older primary children in analysing written materials for examples of sexism and racism. One of the best ways to start is by choosing one of those geography books from the mid 1950s, with pictures of a 'typical English boy and girl'. The boy with his shorts on is enough to persuade most children that times have changed and that we should not identify all British children as being like that. Once this is agreed, the next step of considering children from other countries is quite easy. The seeds of doubt have been sown.

Parents and adults other than teachers can be involved in this, as it provides a good opportunity to discuss criteria for buying resources, both inside and outside school.

Checklists

Older primary pupils can use a checklist similar to that on page 39 to examine written materials in classrooms and libraries. This enables them to develop a healthy scepticism towards the written word.

Hints for discussion

Discuss with the children what makes a good read, and what does not. The patterns of story making can be discussed at a very early stage. Fairy tales are an ideal medium, since the characters are so predictable. Challenging this can provide an opportunity for children to develop a deeper insight into stories. For example, *The Paper Bag Princess*, by Robert Munsch, tells the story of a prince, a princess and a dragon. You can begin by asking the children what they expect of these characters. This can be done orally or written down.

When the story has been read, it is obvious that the children's expectations of the prince and princess have not been fulfilled and the outcome of the story is not as expected. Princess Elizabeth, in fact, rescues Prince Ronald.

'There was Prince Ronald.
He looked at her and said, ''Elizabeth, you are a mess!
You smell like ashes, your hair is all tangled and you are
wearing a dirty old paper bag. Come back when you are
dressed like a real princess.''
'''Ronald,'' said Elizabeth, ''your clothes are really pretty
and your hair is very neat. You look like a prince, but
you are a toad.''
'They didn't get married after all.'

When I have read this with reception children, they have insisted that the prince does marry the princess. Despite the words, their own internal readings are that princes and princesses do get married. Middle infants, however, understood the joke. Their level of understanding reached beyond the actual to being able to understand a complex twist of events. The same story read to seven- to eleven-year-old children in assembly was greeted with great laughter and an understanding that we were looking behind such stories.

It is also interesting to discuss with the children what makes a princess or a prince. Children will quickly tell you that a princess is beautiful with long, blonde hair and blue eyes. The Princess of Wales has perpetuated this image in some ways, as children often point out that a princess 'like Lady Di' has blonde hair. Children often look relieved when you point out that people who do not fit these criteria are not inferior beings!

Discussing with boys the criteria for being a prince results in a similar reaction. It is easy to believe that children are very aware and streetwise and do not think that they are princes and princesses, but actually discuss the issue and it is quite fascinating to note the reactions you get from them. It was also interesting to note the difficulty that many children have in distinguishing between a fairy story and general fiction at many levels in primary school.

The final definition of a good story is when both adults and children can enjoy it. *The Paper Bag Princess* also goes down well on in-service courses, when teachers can laugh about the fact that many of us have at one time or another been looking for a prince or princess, and maturity comes when we recognise that we will have to settle for less – despite having kissed a few toads in the meantime!

There are many stories that take this line. Letterbox Library (see Resources) have an excellent stock of such material.

Drama

Drama is an important medium through which many of these ideas can be explored, both with children and with colleagues. At one level, ideas can be taken from fairy stories for the children to adapt into 'modern fairy stories'. It is also possible to explore more directly the whole idea of stereotyping – what is it to be a giant, a dwarf, a fighter, a nurse? What does it feel like?

Writing

The National Writing Project has made several suggestions which involve children in investigating writing patterns outside as well as inside school.

In Manchester, teachers prepared a questionnaire for parents and other adults looking after nursery and reception children at home. The purpose was to find out about their writing experiences, both past and present. All questionnaires were returned anonymously to school; adults were asked to indicate whether they were male or female and what kinds of writing they did at home and how frequently. Women, it appeared, were far more likely to write messages, letters and shopping lists, and men were more likely to engage in writing that was work-related. The Manchester team felt that this explained an apparent discrepancy: the adults reported that they remembered seeing their mothers write more than their fathers, yet they believed that in their own household both wrote equally. The kinds of writing activity engaged in by women are the kinds that are more likely to be carried out at home and seen by children.

One primary teacher used the book *The Turbulent Term of Tyke Tiler* by Gene Kemp to explore with her class how adults write about boys and girls. Tyke is portrayed throughout the book as someone who has adventures and does dangerous and exciting things. The implicit assumption is that Tyke is a boy. Only at the end is it made clear that Tyke is in fact a girl.

The teacher followed this up by getting her class to talk about their perceptions of gender roles and their responses to them. They explored jobs which they saw as female and those which they saw as male. The children drew on this to examine traditional fairy tales, comics, advertisements and other sorts of writing, and were encouraged to write their own fairy stories.

Knowledge about language

One method of building up children's confidence in language is to let them play with it. Young children who can tell jokes with understanding are usually fairly confident in their ability to manipulate words and make visual pictures for their listeners. It is possible to extend this sort of facility into gender issues in language by getting children to discuss the nouns which are gender-specific – i.e. milkman, dinner lady, spaceman. Then ask them to give alternatives which could be used to describe both women and men doing the same job.

Another exercise can involve examining adjectives. Class teachers can provide children with a list of words similar to the one on page 57, and ask them to put the words into columns according to whether they think they can be used to describe boys, girls or both.

Exercises of this kind need to be handled with care, or they can reinforce stereotypes. Children may be inclined to provide what they think the teacher wants.

Dorothy Walker's *Gender Equality Resource Pack* (see Resources) has several other language-based ideas to try with children, but as with all worksheets, it is important to make sure that they are not just dished out to pupils, but discussed and used with care.

Language and citizenship

Learning how others use language is an important development in children's knowledge about language. Under the National Curriculum, citizenship is a cross-curricular theme, and it is important that children understand the link between language and citizenship. Helping children to become aware of how the language of advertisements is written helps develop not only language awareness, but also a healthy cynicism about advertising copy.

Magazines and comics are one possible area in which to start. It is surprising how many children have difficulty at the beginning in recognising what is and what is not an advertisement. The purpose of advertisements can be discussed, and then the images created by the writing and illustrations can be considered. Gender, race and age stereotypes are often used so blatantly in advertisements that most children can learn fairly quickly how to identify them.

Television advertisements also provide an excellent basis for discussion. The ones shown just before Christmas are particularly good as so many of them are aimed at persuading children to get their parents/Father Christmas to give them toys for Christmas. The play value of different toys can be discussed, and data drawn up about favourite toys. A sympathetic classroom environment can produce a surprising number of 'cross-sex' preferred toys, showing that peer group pressure may be less stereotyped than is sometimes thought.

The quotation at the start of this chapter expresses the belief that through manipulation of language children and adults can control their own worlds. Gusdorf may have used words which excluded women, but the message given by his words is a healthy one.

RESOURCES

Government publications

DES (1975) *A Language for Life* (Bullock Report) (HMSO).

DES (1978) *Primary Education in England* (HMSO).

DES (1988) *Report of the Committee of Inquiry into the Teaching of English Language* (The Kingman Report) (HMSO).

DES (1988) *English for Ages 5 to 11* (the first Cox Report) (HMSO).

DES (1989) *English for Ages 5 to 16* (the second Cox Report) (HMSO).

EOC (1985) *An Equal Start* (Equal Opportunities Commission).

SCDC (1987) *Genderwatch!* (SCDC Publications).

National Writing Project (1990) *What are writers made of?* (Nelson).

NCC (1989) *Curriculum Guidance 1: A Framework for the Primary Curriculum.*

LEA publications

Brent LEA (1985) *Steps to Equality.*

ILEA (1984) *Changing Stores.*

ILEA (1985) *English Curriculum: Gender.*

ILEA (1986) *Primary Matters.*

ILEA (1986) *Language and Gender* in the series *Language Matters* (ILEA Centre for Language in Primary Education).

ILEA (1989) *The Primary Language Record.*

Manchester LEA, Kathy Joyce *Sex Stereotyping explored through Drama.*

Other organisations

Development Education Centre (1986) *Hidden Messages: activities for exploring bias* (Birmingham Development Education Centre, Selly Oak Colleges, Bristol Road, Birmingham).

Masheder, M. (1986) *Let's Co-operate* (Peace Education Project).

National Association for the Teaching of English (1985) *Alice in Genderland* (NATE).

NATE (1985) *Gender Issues in English Coursework* (NATE).

Letterbox Library, 8 Bradbury Street, London N16 8JN (Bookclub which specialises in non-sexist and multicultural books for children, providing good discounts on hardbacks. There is also available a range of inexpensive paperbacks.)

Books for children

Kemp, G. (1977) *The Turbulent Term of Tyke Tyler* (Faber/Puffin).

Munsch, R. (1980) *The Paper Bag Princess* (Hippo Books).

General books

Dixon, B. (1977) *Catching Them Young Vol 1: Sex, Race and Class in Children's Fiction* (Pluto Press).

Dixon, B. (1982) *Now Read On: Recommended Fiction for Young People* (Pluto).

Graddol, D. and Swann, J. (1989) *Gender Voices* (Basil Blackwell).

Hodgeon, J. (1985) *A Woman's World? A report on a project in Cleveland nurseries on sex differentiation in the early years* (Cleveland LEA/Equal Opportunities Commission).

Maccoby, E. and Jacklin, C. (1974) *The Psychology of Sex Differences* (Stanford University Press).

Spender, D. (1980) *Man Made Language* (Routledge and Kegan Paul).

Steedman, C. Urwin, C. and Walkerdine, V. (1985) *Language, Gender and Childhood* (Routledge and Kegan Paul).

Stones, R. (1983) *Pour Out the Cocoa, Janet: sexism in children's books* (Longman/Schools Council).

Walker, D. (1986) *Gender Equality, An Effective Resource for Today's Classroom* (LDA).

Walkerdine, V. and Lucey, H. (1989) *Democracy in the Kitchen* (Virago).

4 MATHEMATICS

A KEY SUBJECT

It is indisputable that mathematics plays an important part in our daily lives, and that a good grounding in mathematics should be an essential educational outcome for all pupils. For the individual pupil, mathematics can be personally and intellectually rewarding and can provide a wide range of career options.

Looking at the current needs of society, it is obvious that there is an increased demand for mathematical knowledge.

• Mathematical language provides a framework for science subjects in school as well as for home economics, technology and geography.

• Mathematical language provides a means of communication, not only for the disciplines it traditionally serves, such as physics and chemistry, but also for social scientists, who can be found in a wide range of occupations.

• Courses and jobs which in the past did not require mathematics as an entry qualification now do. Teaching itself is a good example.

• The economy needs an increased output of mathematics graduates moving into a range of jobs.

• Increased output of such graduates is impossible without a strong, mathematically competent teaching force in the schools, colleges and universities.

The shortage of school-leavers and graduates with the necessary mathematical competence has brought about careful examination of mathematics teaching in schools. The 1982 Cockcroft Report *Mathematics Counts* heralded a new dawn in terms of in-service and initial teacher training in mathematics. It also formally identified the differences in mathematical outcomes for boys and girls in the UK. In Appendix 2 of the Report Hilary Shuard provided an overview of the research to date, which indicated that fewer girls than boys were becoming mathematically competent. Since then, work by researchers and teachers has shown that the problems are extremely complex and that in relation to mathematical skills, concepts and attitudes, gender issues are important from a very early age.

Since the Cockcroft Report, several other organisations have published reports providing information and commenting on gender issues in the learning of mathematics.

• The Girls and Mathematics Association (GAMMA) holds regional and national conferences and produces regular newsletters.

• The Assessment of Performance Unit has published the results of surveys into mathematical development which have raised gender issues.

• The Royal Society, in conjunction with the Institute of Mathematics and its Applications, has published *Girls and Mathematics*, which contains useful statistical information and puts forward some theories to explain why girls are still underachieving in mathematics.

• The Open University has produced a teaching pack entitled *Girls into Mathematics*, which is aimed at in-service work for secondary teachers. A book accompanying this, *Girls Into Maths Can Go*, contains several articles relating to primary mathematics.

• The final report of the National Curriculum Mathematics Working Group included a short section on gender issues, under the heading of equal opportunities. It suggested that a wide variety of modes of assessment should be used, and that teaching materials and examples should be free from gender bias. It summarised the current situation as one in which, 'Although there have been significant improvements in the mathematics attainment of girls, there is still a long way to go'.

• HMI, in its 'Education Observed' series, has produced a publication entitled *Girls Learning Mathematics*, which reports on mathematics teaching in secondary schools, but also has important implications for the primary sector.

Much of the concern about mathematics shortages has concentrated on the participation and achievement of girls in mathematics. In a sense this is a slanted perspective, because it fails to look at the way many boys perceive mathematics. Some data has been collected by the Girls and Mathematics Unit based at the London Institute of Education, which indicates that some boys continue with mathematics to A Level while disliking it considerably.

Girls with similar attitudes 'have been allowed' to give it up, but pressures on boys have made them continue in an area of the curriculum with which they are far from happy. Genuine equality of opportunity means not only enabling girls to take up subjects like mathematics, but also allowing boys to drop these subjects if they wish, without developing a sense of failure.

In the past, the apparent lack of mathematical achievement by girls had been diagnosed from the O Level results, from which it could be seen that a greater percentage of boys entered for and passed O Level mathematics. During the 1980s this trend seemed to be slowing down, partly no doubt because of an increased awareness of the importance of mathematics for both boys and girls.

• In 1985 boys formed 52 per cent of the entry to O Level and 60 per cent of these gained grades A to C as opposed to 52 per cent of the girls.

• The differences were more pronounced at A Level. Only 25 per cent of girls were studying mathematics, compared with 51 per cent of boys. The girls' pass rates were marginally higher.

Few people now believe that these differences are caused by some sort of genetic inferiority. Educationists and politicians have concentrated their attention on different aspects of mathematical education. Some have looked at the performance of girls and boys at different stages in their school careers and related this to their differing attitudes to the subject. Others have reviewed the learning materials provided in schools. Very few have tried to give an overview of the nature of mathematics teaching in relation to children's real-life experiences, although good primary mathematics teaching does try to do exactly that.

This chapter will examine the evidence about the differing performance and attitudes of boys and girls in relation to mathematics, and then it will look at how these differences have been explained. Work done on primary school mathematics texts will be examined, and finally there will be a review of some of the strategies which those teaching mathematics in primary schools have adopted. Computer technology will also be considered in this chapter, not because it is felt that computers and mathematics necessarily go hand in hand, but because there is considerable evidence to show that mathematics co-ordinators frequently have responsibility for computers.

PERFORMANCE AND ATTITUDE DIFFERENCES

Monitoring overall performance in mathematics at primary level has been virtually impossible, just as it has with English. The introduction of Standard Assessment Tasks will make this possible, although it remains to be seen how the nature of the SATs will affect the data extracted from overall figures.

In the days of the 11-plus, it was widely known that girls' performance in all three areas tested (English, Mathematics and Intelligence) was superior to that of boys. Marks were standardised, so that entry into grammar schools was kept as equal as possible.

Overall findings at eleven disguised some complex and important differences. For example, the Assessment of Performance Unit (APU) analysed the performance of boys and girls in a number of different mathematical topics. Among the most general findings, they found that there was a difference between boys' and girls' patterns of performance. These differences were to be found both in the core aspects of the curriculum and in attitudes to mathematics. Boys seemed to perform better in three sub-categories, the measures (length, area, volume and capacity), applications of number, and rate and ratio. Girls appeared to score higher in computation.

The APU also noted differences in attitudes between boys and girls when they were eleven. They found little difference in the level of girls' and boys' enjoyment of mathematics or in their perception of its usefulness, but found that there were considerable differences in their opinions on how difficult they found mathematics.

Statement	Boy/ Girl	Agree %	Uncertain %	Disagree %
I often get into difficulties with maths	B	46	26	28
	G	54	27	19
I am surprised if I get a lot of maths right	B	51	19	30
	G	59	20	21
Maths often gets too complicated for me	B	32	29	39
	G	38	33	29
I don't think maths is difficult	B	32	39	29
	G	24	48	28

(Table taken from *Girls and Mathematics*, published by the Royal Society and the Institute of Mathematics and its Applications)

The APU survey also found that '...girls consistently underrated their performance in relation to their actual attainments and boys consistently overrated their performance – the boys thought they had done better than their results indicated'. (GAMMA Newsletter, March 1983, p 7).

The Royal Society suggested that when children enter secondary schools a greater proportion of boys than girls are likely to arrive expecting to be successful in mathematics. Many girls start their secondary school careers feeling that they have already failed at the subject.

In Appendix 2 of the Cockcroft Report, Hilary Shuard reported on the differences in mathematical performance between boys and girls. Although most of her conclusions are based on research about pupils in secondary schools, she did point out that APU primary surveys confirmed that there was a comparative lack of mathematical confidence in girls as young as eleven. She was surprised that despite the large amount of research about sex differences in mathematics, particularly from the USA, very little evidence was submitted to the committee relating to this topic. The Cockcroft Report's 'Committee for Girls' pointed out in its evidence that the debate on standards in mathematics often seemed to be directed towards boys. Shuard suggested that teachers should ensure that girls receive additional help and encouragement in the areas of measuring, spatial and diagrammatic work, problem solving and place value. Girls, she felt, should be encouraged to tackle higher cognitive level tasks.

BIOLOGICAL, SOCIAL AND CULTURAL PERSPECTIVES

Performance in mathematics

In the past, biological explanations were given for girls' alleged poorer mathematical performance. In the nineteenth century, biological reasons were often given for not allowing girls in Britain to study mathematics.

'Nature herself prescribed to the woman her function as mother and housewife and that law of nature cannot be ignored ... without grave damage, which ... would especially manifest itself in the following generation.' (Max Planck, about 1897).

Until recently, the three most common biological explanations for sex differences in mathematics were:

- a recessive gene on the X-chromosome that increases spatial ability in half of the male and a quarter of the female population;
- a hormonal difference;
- different brain lateralisation in males and females.

The report from the Royal Society cited above, *Girls and Mathematics*, suggested that because the sex differences in mathematical achievement are small at primary level, and become important only during secondary schooling, it was less likely that they could be ascribed to innate biological differences.

Interestingly enough, significant differences in spatial skills have been found only at the lowest level of mathematical participation, and are usually compensated by verbal skills. Where women have had the opportunity to study sufficient mathematics, any deficiency in spatial skills has tended to disappear. This finding has important implications for primary teachers, as it suggests that if young children can be identified as having weak spatial skills, then they need extra practice in order to improve them.

There are many non-biological factors that may explain girls' apparent underachievement in mathematics, and these have been explored at length.

Different play experiences

The cultural and societal environment in which children grow up has a significant effect on the expectations they develop. Influences outside school may affect the mathematically-linked skills required at school. For example, the Royal Society, among others, has suggested that the traditionally masculine toys bought for boys were varied, complex and expensive, whereas traditional female toys were simpler and encouraged passive and solitary activities. They felt that this strengthened masculine and feminine roles, which in the case of girls may not be helpful for developing mathematical ability.

Masculine image of mathematics

Scientific and technological subjects presuppose mathematical knowledge. These subjects have been regarded as of special interest to boys and of relevance to their future roles in society. This is why mathematics was seen as being especially important for boys and men.

> 'Many people, on hearing the words 'female mathematician', conjure up an image of a six-foot, grey-haired, tweed-suited Oxford clad woman ... this image, of course, doesn't attract the young woman who is continually being bombarded with messages ... to be beautiful, 'feminine', and to catch a man.'
> (Professor Martha Smith, contemporary American, as quoted in Harding, 1986).

Confidence as mathematicians

Until recently it was possible to qualify as a teacher without a mathematics O Level. Many primary teachers, with and without this qualification, lack confidence in their own mathematical ability. This anxiety may be passed on to pupils. As the majority of primary teachers are women, girls may also interpret this anxiety about mathematics as part of being an adult woman.

The Girls and Mathematics Unit at the London Institute of Education has, over a period of ten years, carried out detailed theoretical and empirical investigations in this area. In their latest review of the research evidence, *Counting Girls Out*, they take issue with many of the assurances made about girls and mathematics.

An earlier study, *Girls and Mathematics – The Early Years*, found that throughout childhood boys play more with constructional toys and take part in more physical games, which may help to promote spatial awareness and problem solving. The study found that boys were encouraged to be more independent, and suggested that this was a valuable characteristic for problem solving.

Other socialisation patterns may have consequences for later mathematics learning in school. The Girls and Mathematics Unit concluded that more attention needs to be paid to mathematics as a school discipline, to its relationship to the ways girls perceived their situation both at school and in the wider society, and to ways of resolving the contradictions which arise.

The unit's later work has re-examined the relationship between evidence and explanation. Research suggested that girls are actually prevented from learning and acquiring good mathematical experiences, and that this happens early on in primary school. The unit's findings suggested that even when girls are doing well, they are not credited, whereas boys are credited even when performing badly. This may be because the areas of mathematics in which girls perform well, such as computation and number skills, are often considered to be less important than those in which boys do well. When girls do not do well, this is often put down to personal failure or lack of intelligence. It is important, then, that teachers help girls to recognise that their success in mathematics is a result of mathematical ability, and not a matter of sheer hard work and good luck.

Use of computers

Despite its fairly recent introduction into the curriculum, computing already has a male aura. A recent newspaper article reported the Education Secretary's criticism of schools for 'old-fashioned gender stereotyping' which prevented girls from taking up careers in computing. The report noted that between 1986 and 1988 nearly twice as many boys as girls gained an O Level or GCSE in computing, and at A Level the difference was even greater. The percentage of women computer science undergraduates has in fact fallen since the widespread introduction of computers into schools. An early report on computers in the primary curriculum (Burton, 1986) noted the discrepancy:

'There are increasing signs that computers are being used more by boys and male teachers than by girls and female teachers. Primary schools may need to take positive steps to ensure that both sexes have equal opportunities.'

The (NCC) Non-Statutory Guidance for Information Technol sets out the following recommendations for schools.

'5.1 All pupils, regardless of race or gender, should have the opportunity to develop IT capability.
• Statistics show that:
   – more boys than girls use computers;
   – parents are more likely to buy a home computer for boys than girls;
   – computer games are aimed at a male market.
• Boys often see computing as an interesting hobby and so become familiar with the technology and use jargon which is discouraging to those unfamiliar with it.

• In many secondary schools those teaching IT are male.
• In mixed schools boys often dominate computer activities.
• Research shows that girls work better with computers when they set their own goals and work together, rather than in competition.

5.2 Girls are encouraged by:
• seeing women teachers using IT confidently;
• women teachers as IT co-ordinators;
• classroom management which provides equal access to computers;
• curriculum materials and software which are not gender biased;
• using IT for things which interest them.'

As with mathematics and, as we shall see later, science, the arguments about the effects of early socialisation and cultural processes on children's dealings with computers have been affected to a great extent by the introduction of microtechnology into primary schools.

Early socialisation

Anita Straker, while she was Director of the Microelectronics Education Programme, wrote of the urgent need to attract girls to microtechnology. She conducted a sample survey covering the North of England, East Midlands and Home Counties to look at home ownership of calculators, digital watches and computers among top infants and third year juniors. Over 4000 children were involved, and the trend seemed to be the same in all areas.

Twice as many boys as girls had access to a microcomputer at home; nearly twice as many had a calculator; far more boys than girls had a digital watch. The group of children least likely to have any of these gadgets were girls who were single children or who had only sisters.

Anita Straker felt concerned that children who came to school having already played at home with 'wheeled vehicles, clockwork or battery powered toys, a calculator or computer' were more likely to enjoy and benefit from the technological, scientific and mathematical experiences they would have in school.

She made three suggestions for teachers to take up with their classes:

• discuss the problem with the children themselves;

• supervise computer activities to ensure that boys and girls have equal amounts of time at the keyboard, with perhaps girls taking the first turn;

• ensure that any technological problem undertaken is of interest to children of both sexes.

The following chart is taken from the MEP Primary Project Sample Survey (1985), quoted in *Girls Into Maths Can Go* (Burton, 1986). A total of 1926 six- to seven-year-olds and 2186 nine- to ten-year-olds took part in the survey.

Top infants survey	Girls from girls-only families	Girls from mixed families	Boys from mixed families	Boys from boys-only families
Owning their own calculator	18%	26%	35%	36%
Having a calculator in the family	52%	73%	71%	70%
Owning a digital watch	28%	31%	67%	64%
Having a computer in the family	19%	25%	39%	42%
Third year juniors survey	**Girls from girls-only families**	**Girls from mixed families**	**Boys from mixed families**	**Boys from boys-only families**
Owning their own calculator	28%	29%	54%	58%
Having a calculator in the family	66%	72%	74%	72%
Owning a digital watch	51%	55%	79%	80%
Having a computer in the family	27%	36%	48%	59%

Computers seen as a male preserve

A survey that looked at the use of computers in primary schools in Kent indicated that there was another factor which may make pupils think that computers are a male preserve. Here it seemed that sex differences in attitudes towards computers were a by-product of the way computers had been introduced into the schools. The stereotype linking men and computers was being reinforced in the minds of both children and teachers, since so many of the teachers with responsibility for computers were men. It also seems possible that, if only boys are allowed to move computers around the school, additional messages are being sent.

Girls pushed out

Tony Ballarini, writing in *Primary Teaching and Micros*, observed a group of five children constructing a model bell-tower with a hoist which they were planning to control from the microcomputer. He commented that the girls were 'bustled' out of the way, leaving the boys to busy themselves with the engine and subsequent computer control. Once the girls were 'invited' back to use the machine, they were as interested in the activity as the boys.

Ballarini's observations have been backed up by the findings of others. For example, an HMI commenting on the impact of computers in one junior school reported that the pupils are so enthusiastic that 'the girls' ribs are being bruised by the boys, because they are being pushed out of the way in the rush'. From the tone of the report, it is doubtful if the HMI had thought through the implications of this, because he was reported as saying that this was marvellous, and a good example of 'micro fanatics'.

Computers as a branch of technology

Ballarini felt that one reason for the difference in attitude between girls and boys might be that girls did not have access to technical construction kits at home, and might feel disadvantaged when faced with technological problems at school, simply because they were unused to hinges, geared wheels, motors etc. He suggested that the reason why boys were more likely to have access to technical and mechanical toys at home was probably to do with social tradition, and that change would be a slow process.

Available software

The software available for home computers is heavily male-orientated, featuring war games and boys' sports. When a programme does have an identifiable central character, it is nearly always male. Although this is undoubtedly off-putting for many girls, it also needs questioning in relation to boys' experiences. If early computing experiences are concentrated on the mindless destruction of unseen enemies, this is not a particularly healthy trend. It is unlikely to encourage boys to settle to the more varied curriculum-directed computing experiences provided in school.

Differing learning approaches

A small-scale survey examining how eight- and nine-year-old boys and girls tackled Logo for the first time indicated that groups of boys would experiment and try things out, learning from their mistakes on the computer as they went on. Groups of girls, on the other hand, tended to try to work out what would happen before having a go on the computer.

Similar findings were made by a London primary teacher when Big Trak arrived in her school. Everyone wanted to have a turn, yet somehow the boys seemed to be able to get more time on the machine by having a surreptitious go with it when no one was looking!

Classroom-based research such as this needs to be extended and followed through, as there may be important cognitive learning patterns involved which both boys and girls are failing to use properly when faced with new technology.

CURRICULUM CONTENT

Since 1975 we have seen a huge increase in the use of published mathematics schemes in primary schools. Until quite recently, the non-mathematical content of these schemes had been examined in much less detail than that of reading schemes – the implication being, perhaps, that mathematical content was all-important, and writing and illustrations took second place. The language of many early mathematics texts was extremely complex, however, and as teachers became aware of the problems this could cause, it was realised that a successful scheme needed to be at the right literacy level for the children concerned as well as being mathematically correct. The criteria which were introduced for choosing and examining resources in other areas of the curriculum have recently been extended to mathematics.

An early examination of five popular primary mathematics texts, published in the 1970s, concluded that they had a marked sexist bias. Mathematical skills became increasingly defined as masculine as children moved through junior and middle schools. The presence of girls in texts gradually faded, and this seemed to parallel the decline in girls' involvement and achievement in mathematics between infant school and GCE O and A Levels. Similar comments were made about the invisibility of ethnic minority children and their lifestyles.

In 1985 a group of inspectors, advisers and primary teachers in the Inner London Education Authority (ILEA) looked more generally for bias and insensitivity in primary mathematics materials. The resulting publication, *Everyone Counts*, looked at how the issues of class, race, gender and special needs were handled in mathematics books. Few existing schemes came out well from their assessment, but the booklet provided valuable criteria for assessing materials, and suggested ways of taking action by looking at materials in school and raising children's awareness of bias and insensitivity. Editors of more recent mathematics texts are far more aware of the need to correct bias.

Several writers have suggested that there is a mismatch between the 'ideal' mathematics learner, who is naturally inquisitive, and the ideal pupil who may be more passive and dependent. The early Nuffield guides to mathematics – *The First Three Years* – gave as their criteria for developmental progress terms such as 'helps with activities' and 'understands simple instructions'. These could be seen as stereotypically feminine, assuming an obedience and compliance which does not correspond to the ideal for mathematical children, 'who must be set free to make discoveries and think for themselves'.

Much of the work on gender issues in mathematics has been done at secondary level, and it would be easy for primary teachers to feel that the problems lie there, rather than in the primary school. However, if children are spending seven years doing mathematics in primary school we must ensure that negative gender-related performances and attitudes are not being transferred at eleven.

STRATEGIES: WHERE ARE WE NOW?

Existing policy

The first step should be to look at the present mathematics policy document to ensure that the school's policy on equal opportunities permeates its mathematics policy.

Resources

Examine all the resources within the school. This should include unofficial as well as official schemes. Teacher-made workcards and games also need examining. This is a difficult area, particularly if teachers or others have spent a great deal of time making materials. Suggestions for criteria can be found on page 39.

Monitoring classroom interaction

Detailed planning for this can be found in the previous chapter (pages 59 to 61). There are, however, particular aspects of classroom interaction which relate to the mathematics curriculum.

Scarcity of resources

Shortage of resources can place an increased burden on pupils, as they must share and wait for their turn.

Extending play experiences

Early play activities need monitoring carefully to ensure that as soon as children come into schools their play and learning experiences are extended rather than reinforced in a stereotyped way. This can raise some very real difficulties in nurseries and infant classrooms in which the children themselves plan their morning's activities. It can severely limit a timid child's experiences, if he or she chooses familiar and safe activities every day.

Team-work

Mathematical activities need reviewing in terms of gender-related issues when they involve working as a whole class, working in groups, or working in pairs.

Observing activities

Are there any gender-related issues involved when pupils are engaged in activities such as:
- investigating;
- practising skills;
- using apparatus;
- asking for help?

Language

Do some pupils only gain praise for non-mathematical achievements; for example, for being neat and tidy? These characteristics are important, but they can result in pupils spending too much time on the appearance rather than the content of their work. Evidence from secondary schools shows that this is a particular problem with some girls.

Computers

Because of the chronic shortage of computers in primary schools, pupils who are entirely dependent on school for their experience of computing will get very little, and may lack confidence. If children always work co-operatively, either in pairs or in a small group, they may be able to disguise the fact that they are not interacting at all with the machine.

A one-to-one session with the computer can produce some interesting findings. *Podd* is a particularly good program for this, as it can involve group discussion for the input, but each child can make an individual number of inputs.

WHERE DO WE WANT TO BE, AND HOW DO WE GET THERE?

One possible goal to aim for would be the creation of a school environment in which all the children can enjoy and take part confidently in all mathematical and computing activities.

Many of the strategies identified for achieving the equivalent goal in English are also applicable to mathematics. Monitoring and assessing exactly what is going on in the classroom is the first stage in determining what, if anything, needs to be done.

Much of the literature on gender issues and mathematics tends to suggest innate inadequacies as reasons for girls' learning behaviour. Like all deficit models, this is dangerous, as we risk creating the situation we expect to find. The reasons for some girls' underachievement in mathematics at secondary level are complex. It is important to have high expectations of all pupils, just as it is to acknowledge that some of the experiences gained by some pupils outside school may help them learn mathematics and familiarise them with new technology such as computers.

A deficit model of girls' play activities also fails to acknowledge that many of the play activities in which girls often take part may be of help in developing concepts, skills and attitudes related to co-operation, caring and sharing. These are important , and should be encouraged in all pupils.

The strategies suggested here have been successfully carried out over a period of time in different primary schools. Monitoring the progress of initiatives like these, which are essentially practical and classroom-based, is often extremely difficult. However, some attempt at monitoring must be made if change is to be recorded as part of the overall evaluation of what is going on in any one class or school.

Discussion

If the review shows up an area for concern, discuss this with the children. Many of the issues likely to be involved are an essential part of any personal and social education (PSE) policy, i.e. polite behaviour, sharing and taking turns.

A 'tinkering table'

Provide and monitor the use of a 'tinkering table', so that pupils who do not have the opportunity to develop particular skills at home can do so at school. If the

classroom is too small to have such a table, a box can be provided, so that suitable items can be provided as a 'structured free choice' activity. Items for the tinkering table can vary, and will depend on the age and maturity of the children, but you might include some of the following:

- a broken watch or clock;
- a radio;
- a unit from a washing machine;
- a plug;
- screwdrivers of different sizes.

Some children seem to have an endless supply of such items that they can bring from home. It is important to ensure that those who show little interest do become involved – the inside of a broken talking doll worked for one child!

A toy survey

Examine the play value of different toys. With the children, look at television advertisements which are aimed at making them persuade their parents to buy particular toys. (The period leading up to Christmas is a good time for this!) The objectives of this exercise are various, but as far as mathematics is concerned it can be seen as a means of widening young children's toy choices.

Ensuring access

Try to ensure that there is a good supply of the necessary equipment, so that pupils are not forced into sharing apparatus unnecessarily. Locating additional items can be made easier if you have a good school stock list.

Extra practice

Just as extra help is given to children with reading problems, so early mathematical difficulties need to be identified and resolved. Additional practice with practical activities such as weighing and measuring (AT 8) and spatial work (ATs 10 and 11) is one way of doing this, particularly if another adult can be drawn in to help.

Mathematics as a reward

It is important to have mathematical equipment easily available, so that children can 'choose' to experiment with it if they wish. In some classrooms, children are invited to read if they finish a set task early. Providing a free-choice mathematical experience as another option can widen horizons.

Careers

Extend the children's knowledge of careers that require mathematics. *Careers education and guidance from 5 to 16* urges teachers to ensure careers education for children, regardless of aptitude, ability, sex or ethnic background.

One way in which this can be done is to examine the mathematical skills which are needed for different occupations in various areas of work. There are several picture packs now available which provide photographs of men and women in non-traditional occupations. This in itself should help address some of the issues related to cross-curricular themes such as economic and industrial awareness. An analysis of the work of a bricklayer or a dress designer shows how they both need a variety of mathematical skills, including computation, measuring, estimating and predicting. The *Working Now* pack (see Resources) contains 16 useful photographs, as well as teachers' notes for exploring gender roles in the primary classroom.

Help with computers

If some pupils do seem to be getting pushed away from computers, then some form of support is needed.
• If the reason seems to be that they just are not interested, then a programme review may help – perhaps involving the children concerned.
• If one group of children is dominating the sessions, then different groupings may help.
• At one stage, I ran a computer club at the same time as the after-school football session. This resulted in the attendance of a large number of girls, who did become far more confident about computer use.

• Ensure that it is not always men and boys who are seen handling and moving the computers.

• Provide programmable toys. Many more so-called 'boys' toys' have this facility than those usually given to girls, which enables boys to gain experience of manipulating machines. Using programmable toys in the classroom extends these experiences to other children, and it also provides a way of ensuring that children whose families cannot afford such expensive toys have an opportunity to play with them.

These strategies are simply a matter of good practice, and many primary teachers already provide the extensive mathematical experiences needed to help all pupils achieve their full potential within the National Curriculum. Reviewing and monitoring are important factors in ensuring that all pupils take up what is offered and do not opt out of extending their mathematical and technological skills at an early age.

RESOURCES

Government publications

Department of Education and Science (1982) *Mathematics Counts* (the Cockcroft Report) (HMSO).
DES (1989) *Girls Learning Mathematics* (DES).
DES (1989) *Mathematics in the National Curriculum* (HMSO).
DES (1990) *Technology in the National Curriculum* (HMSO).
Ellis, J. (1986) *Equal Opportunities and Computer Education in the Primary School* (Equal Opportunities Commission).
HMI (1988) *Careers education and guidance from 5 to 16* (HMSO).

LEA Publications

ILEA (1985) *Primary Matters: Some Approaches to Equal Opportunities in Primary Schools*.
Wigan ILEA (1989) *Gender Differences in Spatial Ability in the First School*.

Publications from other organisations

Development Education Centre (1989) *Working Now* (DEC).
Economic and Social Research Council *Girls and Mathematics: Some Lessons for the Classroom* (ESRC).
The Royal Society and The Institute of Mathematics and its Applications (1986) *Girls and Mathematics* (The Royal Society).

General

Ballerini, T. (1985) 'Ding Dong Bell', in *Primary Teaching and Micros* (March).

Blinke, J. (1987) 'Girls and Mathematics' in *Junior Education* (February).

Burton, L. (1986) *Girls Into Maths Can Go* (Cassell).

Mosley, F. (1985) *Everyone Counts - looking for bias and insensitivity in primary mathematics materials* (Harcourt Brace Jovanovich)

Eddowes, M. (1983) *Humble Pi* (Longman).

Harding, J. (ed) (1986) *Perspectives on Gender and Science* (Falmer Press).

Hoyles, C. (1986) *Girls and Computers* (University of London Bedford Way Papers No. 34).

Northam, J. (1982) 'Girls and boys in primary maths books' in *Education 3-13* No. 10.

Spencer, Diane 'Girls put off computers by school stereotyping' in *The Times Industrial Supplement*, 13.7.90.

Straker, A. (1985) 'Positive Steps' in *The Times Educational Supplement*, 5.4.85.

Walden, R. & Walkerdine, V. (1982) *Girls and Mathematics: From Primary to Secondary Schooling* (University of London Bedford Way Papers, No. 24).

Walkerdine, V. (1989) *Counting Girls Out* (Virago).

5 SCIENCE

THE NEW 'BASIC'

The National Curriculum has formally acknowledged the importance of primary science. English, mathematics and science are the designated core subjects and the only ones to be assessed formally with Standard Assessment Tasks in primary schools.

To some extent, this is the culmination of changes in primary science teaching over the past twenty years. 'Nature study' in its many forms has always been a part of progressive primary school teaching, but the Schools Council Programme Science 5 to 13 widened the perspectives of science teaching to include foundation elements of chemistry and physics as well as the biology that children would meet in secondary school.

The Final Orders for science, with its 17 attainment targets, marks an important change in emphasis for the primary curriculum. Not only does it confirm the increasing importance of science education in primary schools, but also the large number of attainment targets ensures that schools will have to give science a much heavier time allocation. In schools and LEAs which adopt a thematic approach to whole-school planning, topic work therefore tends to be science-led. This, in turn, has implications for other areas of the curriculum such as the humanities, which are not likely to be assessed formally at primary level.

The Science Working Party acknowledged in their consultation documents that gender issues were an important element in science teaching. They were influenced, no doubt, by the widespread concern during the previous fifteen years over the underachievement of girls and women in science education. In Britain this concern had been highlighted by three fairly disparate groups – science educators, feminists and science-based industry. Since each group had different vested interests, their definitions of the problem and the solutions they suggested varied considerably.

Gender and science education

There have been considerable shifts in the arguments concerning gender and science. Much of the very early work, particularly that carried out in the nineteenth century, was approached from a physiological viewpoint, looking for physical reasons why men were scientists and women were not. Later, a psychological angle to the question was adopted. Put very crudely, this said that if girls did not do physical sciences there must be something wrong with their perception of science, of the world or of themselves. Both the physical and psychological explanations convey the message of a deficit model for girls, i.e. that there is something wrong with them and that is why they do not do science.

A third argument has now been developed which has important implications for primary teachers. This is largely in response to the failure of the other two theories to provide a helpful solution to some of the problems diagnosed. This third approach identifies the problems in three main areas; within science, within the schools, and within society. It argues that the teaching institutions, and science itself, need to change. Science should be seen as a social process, which can and should be linked with the needs of the learner as well as those of society.

Good science guidelines in primary schools should show how National Curriculum attainment targets can be achieved through programmes of study which interest and motivate pupils and also reach set targets. The non-statutory guidance attached to the NCC Final Orders takes this point of view, and hopes that:

'the common, balanced curriculum which pupils will follow will help to eliminate problems of sex imbalance in the uptake of specific science courses. Nevertheless, it is likely that the problems of low expectations of many girls, particularly in a physical sense, will remain. The design of courses, the use of materials which avoid sex stereotyping and the involvement of girls' own perspectives on problems, issues and ideas are important factors in increasing the involvement of girls in physical science.' (7.5)

The Science Working Group felt that the eventual success of this approach would be measured by the uptake of the full, double award science by girls in Key Stage 4.

The advice given for preparing schemes of work suggests, under the heading 'Particular Issues', that consideration be given to both gender and ethnic issues. Sadly, but not surprisingly, little advice is given about exactly what this entails. This chapter, therefore, will look at the information collected about gender issues in science and try to summarise what exactly this means for primary teachers, particularly for science co-ordinators.

The data collected for science tends to reflect the findings for mathematics and, similarly, those who have examined gender issues in relation to science have tended to concentrate on the secondary sector. It has been left largely to primary teachers themselves to look at the beginnings of science learning in nurseries and primary schools and to question gender-related issues. The great advantage of this type of action-based research is that it is fairly easy for class teachers to replicate, so they can base their teaching on findings they have drawn up themselves.

PERFORMANCE AND ATTITUDE DIFFERENCES

As science was not tested in the 11-plus, research has mainly relied on 0 and A Level results. The tables below show the results for 1986-7; the source is the Statistics Unit of the Equal Opportunities Commission.

Attempted CSE/ 0 Level	Girls (thousands)	Boys (thousands)
Biology	199.0	110.2
Chemistry	93.5	121.4
Physics	74.1	189.8
Computer science	76.0	222.1

GCE A Level	Girls (thousands)		Boys (thousands)	
	Attempts	Passes	Attempts	Passes
Physics	7.9	6.0	28.1	21.9
Other sciences	2.1	1.6	6.9	5.6

The introduction of GCSE appears to have had little effect, as shown by the results from the National Examination Authority for GCSE in 1988:

GCSE subject entries	Girls	Boys
Biology	47,536	26,083
Chemistry	32,732	40,469
Physics	22,338	57,552
Science Dual Award	986	1,224
Science Modular	15,824	15,093

The problem in the physical sciences, and to some extent in mathematics, is not that girls do badly when they take these subjects but that they opt out of them in such large numbers.

Statistics like those above show that the drop-out of girls from science courses takes place before the fifth form. One of the concerns of the Science Working Group for the National Curriculum was to try to prevent this, and strong arguments were put forward for having a full science curriculum at Key Stage 4. There is still concern that the eventual decision to provide two separate models for science at Key Stage 4 may result in many pupils choosing the more limited model.

Research workers who have examined gender issues in relation to science have suggested that it is informal barriers that have led to the massive drop-out by girls at secondary level. They have also noted that biology has stayed popular with girls, whereas they have opted out of the physical sciences. This preference for biology showed up in some early research undertaken in primary schools in the 1970s. Here, science attitude tests suggested that girls preferred the biological sciences and boys the physical sciences.

The issues are complex and the data is sometimes conflicting. A survey carried out in 1988 involving 342 children from 15 primary schools in Leicestershire was reported in the Times Educational Supplement. All the children involved were transferring to the same comprehensive school. The study compared the performance and enthusiasm of pupils who had considerable primary science experience with those who did not. This showed that initial interest quickly waned.

The survey recorded a positive increase in girls' interest in both the biological and the physical sciences during their time at primary school and showed that, at the end of the primary phase, many girls indicated a stronger wish than the boys in their class to do more school science. One year later, however, the pattern of the findings had changed considerably, and many girls appeared disillusioned. Those who had done substantial amounts of primary science were among the most disillusioned at this stage.

The Equal Opportunities Commission (EOC) felt that these results did not just mean that secondary schools should change their methodology to one that was more in tune with primary schools. They felt that the issues were complex, and highlighted the lack of science in activities pursued by many girls out of school. The researchers suggested that some form of positive discrimination in primary science could compensate for this.

Professor plod

My professor is now trying to make a qure for the common cold if he does not sec seed he will keep trying

Natalie Cuddy aged 7

Research on the image of science and scientists has examined how boys and girls in primary schools see science. One study invited all 400 pupils in a JMI school to draw a picture of a scientist. The overwhelming response was to draw a white man.

Older children were asked to write about the work of a scientist, and their writing indicated a gender difference in perception. Girls tended to perceive science as an area in which things are done to help people, whereas boys were more excited about the idea of inventions. Many pupils drew scientists looking and behaving in a crazed fashion.

Studies of this sort have been done elsewhere, and the results generally point to an image of science as a male preserve. The pervasive idea of the mad scientist perhaps indicates another aspect of the image of science that needs examining. Replicating such a study is fairly easy for most class teachers to do, and provides an opportunity to discuss stereotypes with the children and with teaching colleagues. It can also provide an ideal opportunity to invite into school some scientists, both female and male, who break the stereotypes. Again, as with mathematics, cross-curricular themes such as economic and industrial awareness can be included.

BIOLOGICAL, SOCIAL AND CULTURAL PERSPECTIVES

Many of the biological misconceptions considered in the chapter on mathematics have also been applied to science. There are various ways in which male scientists have explained the virtual absence of women scientists in the past, and as each theory was discarded, another theory took its place. Similar theories have also been used to explain the alleged inferiority of 'negroes' and the 'lower classes'.

For some years, it has been noted that boys appear to perform better than girls at tests which involve spatial visualisation. It has been argued that visual-spatial skills are essential for the abstract reasoning on which science is based, and that scientific ability is therefore linked to a biological base. As we saw in the chapter on mathematics, in the 1970s it was believed that spatial ability was partly inherited through an X-linked recessive gene found more often in men than in women. More recent data has cast doubt on this hypothesis, but has not completely dismissed all biological explanations.

However, the fact that in other countries large numbers of women study science successfully indicates that other factors must be involved. There is also increasing evidence that girls from particular ethnic minority groups in this country are achieving well in science subjects. Both these factors point to cultural and social influences that may impinge on boys' and girls' learning of science in schools.

This is in effect what the Assessment of Performance Unit survey, *Girls and Physics*, tried to establish. It used data from the USA and the UK to examine the out-of-school activities of pupils aged nine to eleven. The 'Topic' chart below deals with the percentages of nine-year-old boys and girls claiming to have worked or experimented

Topic	% pupils boys	girls	Activity	% pupils boys	girls
Batteries and bulbs	61	47	Make models from a kit (Airfix)	42	6
Magnets	68	57	Play pool, billiards or snooker	59	30
Floating and sinking	58	48	Play with electric toy sets	45	16
Dissolving	55	54	Create models using Lego, etc	50	23
Living animals	65	63	Take things apart to see inside	38	18
Mirror	41	43	Go fishing or pond dipping	30	13
Seeds	61	64	Watch birds	30	27
Living plants	63	68	Sow seeds or grow plants	30	34
Shadows	43	48	Look after small animals/pets	52	57
Sound	55	67	Collect/look at wild flowers	8	27
			Weigh ingredients for cooking	29	60
			Knit or sew	5	46

with particular named topics; it comes from 1982 USA national survey data. The 'Activity' chart deals with percentages of eleven-year-old boys and girls claiming to have 'quite often' engaged in particular activities out of school; this information comes from the 1984 APU national survey data. Both charts are quoted in the APU booklet *Girls and Physics*.

The data showed that boys were likely to have far more out-of-school experience of scientifically-based activities than girls. Many of the boys' experiences involved scientific equipment. A further survey on reading matter outside school showed similar findings.

When asked if they would like to 'do more' of each of the named activities, the enthusiasm of the nine-year-old boys and girls matched the polarisation of their actual choices; in other words, girls wanted more involvement in just those activities in which they were already engaged more often than boys, and vice versa. Corresponding APU surveys of 13- and 15-year-olds produced similar patterns of polarisation.

The APU concluded that, by the age of eleven, boys and girls were already on very divergent paths in terms of scientific interests, which were reflected in their general leisure activities. Already, by eleven, boys showed a greater enthusiasm for finding out 'how things work', with girls interested rather more in the issues of health, the human body and the aesthetic aspects of weather, colour and music. This led to the conclusion that more boys than girls begin formal physics lessons in secondary school with a firm base from which to assimilate new knowledge and understanding. Boys also tend to approach formal practical work in secondary science with greater confidence, enthusiasm and competence than girls in general, possibly because of their more extensive experience of practical activity as young children.

It is perhaps worth asking at this stage whether it matters that boys show more interest in science and, if so, whether primary teachers can do anything about it. The answer lies in what we do about reading, where girls tend to score better than boys and have less difficulty learning to read. We do not use this as a reason for letting boys drop out of reading classes; in fact, most schools operate a policy of positive discrimination and provide extra help for poor readers, help which goes predominantly to boys. The same could be done to boost the science experiences of girls.

The APU findings fit quite neatly with those of the Leicestershire survey referred to on page 98. Girls who had done quite a bit of physical science in school expressed interest in it. This should be a strong indication that many girls need the practical experiences provided at school, in order to become interested in areas that are not covered by their leisure pursuits.

Other researchers have examined the social framework within which science is taught in schools, and some have suggested that girls are hindered scientifically because of the 'femininity of primary schools'. It was argued that primary schools create an environment of 'obedience, silence, passivity and conformity'. This in turn creates a mismatch between the 'ideal learner', who is naturally inquisitive, and the 'ideal pupil', who is passive and fairly silent. This line of argument suggests that boys are ideal learners because they dominate the talking, playground space, choice of toys and so on, which provides them with particular skills useful in developing scientific concepts (such as spatial awareness) and allows them wider experiences to draw on and reflect about. Girls are rewarded for being 'ideal pupils' when they are tidy and quiet, whilst boys are taught to be independent – a most important scientific attitude.

I rather suspect that researchers arguing like this have spent little time in primary schools since their own schooling. Few primary schools today create an environment of 'obedience, silence, passivity and conformity'. Certainly quiet, shy children are at an educational disadvantage since they make fewer demands on the busy teacher, and their learning needs can be lost in a group. Work by the Equal Opportunities Commission on nurseries and infant classes in Northern Ireland indicated that shy, withdrawn pupils are more likely to be girls. It is very much harder to link this to lack of achievement in science, particularly without hard data.

One particular image of femininity can discourage girls from the originality and experimentation which are so important in early scientific work. Most infant teachers will be familiar with the sight of beautifully dressed little girls who are terrified of getting dirty. The long-term effects of always being careful about the state of their clothes may inhibit the curiosity necessary to encourage scientific experimentation.

Another argument used in the past to explain why girls tended to opt out of science in secondary schools was that many secondary science departments were staffed almost entirely by men, and this presented a very male image of science. It was also pointed out that early science work in primary schools tended to be done by male teachers who had had some scientific background themselves, and experiments were rarely from the female sphere of activities. This has changed radically in primary schools over the past few years and may alter the image of science for both boys and girls. The problem still remains, however, for many secondary schools, although there is a much greater degree of awareness than before. The apparent male domination of science teaching is an issue taken up by some primary/secondary liaison schemes when they show female primary teachers working alongside male secondary science teachers.

Work in UK secondary schools by Margaret Spear and Margaret Crossman has revealed the following disturbing information:
• teachers award higher marks on average to work they think is from a boy than to identical work that they think has been produced by a girl;
• secondary teachers feel it is more important for boys than for girls to get qualifications in science;
• teachers show more interaction with boys than with girls.

On this final point it is difficult to know in whose interest this is, as the amount of teacher interaction is most marked when teachers criticise boys. This links with the adult/child interaction noted in the Cleveland nursery schools (page 53).

The lessons for primary teachers are complex. Girls are less likely to meet with scientific and technological experiences outside schoolbecause of differing socialisation patterns. Within school, the very practical nature of primary science means that scarce resources, including the teacher's time, need to be monitored carefully. Pupils who gain a disproportionate amount of time and resources are effectively penalising others, particularly those who are not in a position to obtain similar practical experiences outside school.

CURRICULUM CONTENT

Until the advent of the National Curriculum, it would have been difficult to find out exactly what the curriculum content of any school's science programme was without examining their science guidelines. The Final Orders have changed this, and it is now clear what schools must cover. The teaching methods and styles have also to some extent been determined by the suggested programmes of study. The responses that children make will be largely dependent on their teachers' and their own interests, and it remains to be seen whether any gender issues arise from this more prescriptive approach to primary science.

Research in the past has looked at the content of the science curriculum in terms of textbooks. As with English and mathematics, the content of primary science texts was reviewed in the mid 1970s and found wanting in the imagery it projected. Publications were found to present an overall impression of the maleness of science, and they tended to be orientated towards male interests.

Texts and resources brought out to fit in with the National Curriculum will be unlikely to project stereotyped images, either racist or sexist. The problem occurs, as usual, when schools are forced to use dated resources because of shortage of funds.

The importance of early play experiences has been emphasised fairly consistently in relation to developing scientific and technological concepts and attitudes. For some time now there has been heightened awareness of the need to record and analyse the sorts of play experiences children receive in school. This in itself is evidence of the increased professionalism of all those who work within early years education. The analysis has been followed up with an increased tendency to direct children's play, so that play activities extend their previous experiences rather than reinforcing the familiar. One consequence of this has been that subjective ideas of gender differences in play activities have now been documented with hard data. The table below comes from an unpublished survey by a local authority working party in Manchester in 1981.

Activity	Age group 3-5 (nursery)		Age group 5 and over (infant)	
	% boys	% girls	% boys	% girls
Wendy house/home corner	42	58	34	66
Dolls' house	46	54	22	78
Constructional play	64	36	66	34
Bricks, cars, trains	69	31	73	27

One area about which teachers have shown particular concern is that of constructional play. Most nursery and infant classrooms contain some form of constructional play equipment, such as bricks and Lego. One reason for the provision of such equipment comes from the belief that a wide experience of different types of constructional play equipment provides a good foundation for later scientific, technological and mathematical work.

Monitoring free choice play can provide a means of finding out about curriculum content for young children. However, simply recording play activity is not enough; monitoring should entail analysis as well as observation, as in a recent study in Wigan. The work in Wigan schools involved observation and analysis of Lego play. The analysis included details of language used while playing with Lego. Children worked in single-sex pairs, and were given two tasks. For the first task they were asked to imagine that they were going on a journey in a rocket to a planet they had never visited before. They were asked to imagine what it might be like, and to make a model of something they would see there. Data was collected and analysed for gender similarities and differences in:

• the kinds of models made;
• the range of categories;
• interactions by the children while they were on task.

Findings showed that:

• there was a larger range of categories for boys than for girls;
• there was an overlap of only three categories for boys and girls – these were a house, a car and a tractor;
• There were more interactions by the girls than the boys, with the older girls talking significantly more to their partners than the older boys;
• the boys made a larger range of machines, whereas the girls' models were more concerned with human interest.

Observations on language showed that:

• the boys' language was more technical than the girls';
• the girls' language was largely concerned with human interest, rather than the task in hand;
• the boys were more confident, assertive and competitive, and included more violence in their language;
• the girls were more timid, more imaginative, less competitive and less technical.

The nature of the task involved participation by both boys and girls; however, the language used by the girls was extending their social abilities, while that of the boys was extending the technological and scientific aspects of the task in hand. Both represent important functions for language, but they also show important differences in how boys and girls perceive the same task.

STRATEGIES: WHERE ARE WE NOW?

Existing policy

The existing science policy document should be examined to ensure that equal opportunities issues are taken into account.

Resources

Examine all the resources within the school. Recent publications should reflect good practice, as publishing companies are now very aware of the issues. Even so, do not be complacent. The major problems will arise with:
• older materials, which may often be used by teachers but not displayed openly;
• teacher-made work cards and games;
• dated pictures on boxes containing equipment;
• non-fiction books in class and school libraries;
• display posters.

Monitoring classroom interaction

Detailed planning for this can be found in the English and mathematics chapters.

WHERE DO WE WANT TO BE, AND HOW DO WE GET THERE?

The aim is to create a school where all children progress through the science programmes of study with confidence and enjoyment. There are a number of factors to consider in order to achieve this objective.

Good classroom management

This is a key element if the school's policies are to be carried out properly. Organising practical science activities can be fraught with difficulties for experienced and inexperienced teachers alike. Many primary teachers have had limited scientific education themselves and lack confidence in many of the targeted areas, particularly at Levels 5 and 6. Science co-ordinators can have a particularly difficult task in showing how learning outcomes may result from a wide range of different activities. Areas with a strong advisory curriculum support team at the LEA are in a better position to help class teachers than those where the science co-ordinator is solely responsible for bringing National Curriculum training back into school.

There are now several good published science schemes which have responded to these difficulties. Once the science content becomes familiar, teachers will be better able to respond more directly to the different learning needs of individual children.

A science table

This can be set out as an interactive display, positioned where children can work with it. Studies indicate that pupils with a range of out-of-school science experiences did better at in-school science activities. Providing an opportunity for children to experiment and to test out different types of scientific equipment is one way in which some form of positive discrimination can be given to pupils whose out-of-school experiences lack this dimension. There are several areas where additional activities can be helpful:

- making models;
- playing with electric toy sets;
- taking things apart to see inside;
- weighing ingredients for cooking;
- knitting and sewing.

Sometimes the science table can be used either to reinforce work already going on in class or to extend this work. There are some excellent easy-to-follow science guides available which deal with subjects such as mirrors, feathers and so on. Even older junior children can enjoy following up ideas from books aimed at a much younger age group.

Science kits

One infant school I visited had a construction-only afternoon. To begin with, this had involved collecting a number of different construction kits so that children would have a selection of equipment to try out. Now the tradition is well established, and there is considerable evidence that becoming familiar with the kits has helped children to make for themselves the choice in favour of playing with construction kits at other times.

Photographs

Reinforce for the children the idea that science is for and about them by taking photographs of them as they are carrying out scientific experiments. The photographs can then be used to make a class display.

Single-sex groups

If boys are inclined to dominate mixed groups for science and constructional activities, try arranging the children in single-sex groups. This can either be done without the children being aware of what you are doing, or the matter can be discussed openly.

Role models

Provide a wide range of role models so that all pupils' ideas about what it is to be a scientist can be extended. Increasing pupils' awareness of jobs that require science is an important part of the economic and industrial awareness theme, and is applicable to children at all ages, with differing degrees of awareness. The science element involved in being a dentist, doctor, nurse or midwife, for example, can be shown by looking at the sorts of instruments used in each profession. Talk about how long it takes to train for the different jobs, and discuss too the pleasure of being a student, an idea with which many young children will be unfamiliar.

Older juniors can look more closely at:
• careers which require scientific or technical qualifications , such as vet, teacher, occupational therapist;
• careers involving people's health, such as dentist, doctor, chiropodist, biochemist, ambulance driver, physiotherapist, optician;
• careers where you can meet and help people, such as hairdresser, garage mechanic, driver, telephone engineer;
• careers which are concerned with the home and garden, such as architectural technician, electrician, home economist, plumber, textile technologist, landscape gardener;

• artistic/creative careers, such as fashion designer, graphic designer, artist, printer, jeweller;
• careers which involve working with animals or an interest in nature, such as florist, fish farmer, forestry worker, vet, zoologist.

Even very young children can make an A to Z of careers, looking closely at the many jobs people can do which involve science.

RESOURCES

Government publications

Assessment of Performance Unit (1986) *Girls and Physics* (DES).
Department of Education and Science (1989) *Science in the National Curriculum* (HMSO).
Equal Opportunity Commission (1988) *Facts ... that figure in equal opportunities and education* (EOC).
EOC *We Can Do It Now!*(EOC).
EOC (Ireland) *Gender Differentiation in Infant Classes.*

LEA publications

Brent Curriculum Development Support Unit *Breaking the Circuit – Girls, boys and electronics: a research project.*
Design it, Build it, Use it – Anti-sexist guidelines for using construction kits with children 3-11.
Wigan (1989) *Gender Differences in Spatial Ability in the First School.*

General

Bowden, J. Hartley, K. and Harrison, P. *Science in Action* (Folens).
Harding, J. (ed) (1986) *Perspectives on Gender and Science* (Falmer Press).
Harlen, W. (1985) 'Girls and primary-school science education' in *Prospects*, Vol. XV No. 4.
Kelly, A. (1987) *Science for Girls?* (Open University Press).
Richards, R. (1989) *An Early Start to Nature* (Simon & Schuster).
Richards, R. Collis, N. and Kincaid, D. (1989) *An Early Start to Science* (Simon & Schuster).

Information posters

The Equal Opportunities Commission has produced a series of free posters showing women scientists, which can be used to show how women have been involved in scientific discoveries. There is also a poster pack on the subject of non-traditional careers, which can provide some positive examples for children. Even if the information is beyond the children, it is useful for staff development!

EOC Posters – *Women Scientists* (Caroline Herschel, Jane Wright, Jane Goodall, Rosalind Franklin, Dorothy Hodgkin, Irene Curie).

EOC Posters – *Non-traditional Careers*.

6 THE FOUNDATION SUBJECTS

One result of the National Curriculum has been to create two formal groupings of subjects to be taught in schools. Core subjects – mathematics, English, science and Welsh in Wales – are balanced with foundation subjects of history, geography, technology, music, art, PE and, in secondary schools, a foreign language. In primary schools teachers are expected to assess pupils in all these areas, but the Standard Assessment Tasks apply only to the core subjects. This is likely to ensure these subjects a continued high status in terms of time allocation and staff development.

The gender issues involved in the three core subjects and information technology have been dealt with in earlier chapters; now we can turn to the implications of gender issues for the foundation subjects.

HUMANITIES

Humanities teaching in primary schools has had a very chequered career, with subject headings changing and continual doubt about what is actually meant by the term 'humanities'. In this book, because they are foundation subjects, history and geography are taken to represent humanities. However, 'humanities' does imply more than just two separate disciplines: it is about humanity, about real people living in the past and in the present. This covers a huge range of material, and therefore selection is necessary. Some cross-curricular themes, such as environmental studies and citizenship, have very distinct links with humanities teaching, and aspects of race, gender and special needs should always be taken into account.

There is heavy criticism of the ways in which geography and history have been taught in primary schools. The HMI report, *Aspects of Primary Education: The Teaching and Learning of History and Geography*, found that the majority of schools had great difficulty in making satisfactory provision for history and geography. The subject working parties made a real attempt, despite their limited primary expertise, to provide much stronger support for teachers and to set up a framework for primary history and geography. Both subjects in different ways have provided examples of the gender implications involved in subject areas which concern themselves directly with the human condition.

Geography

Section 8.7 of the final report of the Geography Working Party examines the cross-curricular dimensions of the National Curriculum. In relation to gender issues, they note with concern the evidence that girls are more likely than boys to drop geography after the age of 14. They point out that this may reflect the option structure in some schools, but it might also mean that the subject has not been made sufficiently attractive to girls.

The Working Party feels that the advent of the National Curriculum presents the:

'...opportunity to seek to remedy this particular inequality by providing for a structured development of geographical skills for all pupils from the age of 5. It will be important, however, for teachers to select methodologies and topics which are "girl-friendly" in the sense that they will tend to compensate for any differences in experience – for instance, by encouraging both sexes to explore a range of environments under supervision. So far as possible, assessment methods should give credit for what both girls and boys can do rather than emphasise what one or other sex may find, on average, particularly difficult.' (8.7)

The report continues:

'8.8 In our programme of study we have also sought to prescribe material which will appeal to both sexes. It is, however, not our intention that some geographical topics are for girls, others for boys. Both sexes are entitled to a balanced diet of geography.
8.9 In all our recommendations, we have sought to avoid the use of language which is gender-specific, or examples which give prominence to the work or roles of one sex rather than the other. Much will depend on how material is selected and taught, including the careful

choice of case study material, so as to avoid pupils acquiring (or having reinforced) stereotyped images of men's and women's roles.'
(Geography Working Party, Final Report (8.8))

The primary teacher may well wonder how this can be incorporated into a strategy for teaching in primary schools. The Working Party reflects the widespread concern about gender-related performance and attitude differences in geography. HMI, in *Geography from 5 to 16*, asked teachers to ensure, through 'monitoring and sensitive intervention, that both sexes benefit from participation in appropriate activities'.

There is some evidence to show that girls' underachievement in geography and unwillingness to participate in the subject probably starts much earlier than secondary school. As long ago as 1967, it was noted that by the start of secondary school girls seemed less able to grasp basic geographical concepts than boys of the same age. It was suggested that this might explain their apparent reluctance to study the subject later. Several suggestions have been put forward to explain why girls opt out, and it might be useful for teachers, both primary and secondary, to be aware of some of these so that they are able to gear their teaching towards accommodating additional learning variables.

Environmental knowledge

There does not appear to be any biological reason for the apparent differences in performance and attitude in geography, so it seems likely that such differences are caused by social and cultural factors and different parental attitudes to child-rearing. The Newsoms in 1977 found that parents encouraged their seven-year-old sons to pursue outdoor activities, whereas seven-year-old daughters were encouraged to spend more time indoors. The reason suggested for this was parental fear about dangers for girls outside the home.

Another study looked at a group of children between the ages of six and eleven and found that, from eight onwards, boys travelled further from home. This appeared to influence the quantity and quality of their environmental knowledge, and possibly accounts for their apparently greater ability to present space through mapping skills. It is possible to see how, by the end of primary school, girls may be less likely to succeed in geography because they already show less environmental capability than boys. An emphasis on map work and mapping skills in the secondary school may perpetuate the advantages enjoyed by boys. An additional factor may be that girls develop less curiosity about their environment, because they have less opportunity to explore it.

Curriculum content

In the mid 1980s an ILEA working party evaluated over 40 geography texts, both primary and secondary. They found that almost without exception the books displayed a degree of sexist bias in both content and language. Much human geography was presented as the geography of men, with both illustrations and content either ignoring or under-representing women. It is important that all pupils feel that the subject matter is for and about them – 'girl-friendly', as the Geography Working Party puts it. The ILEA working party found that recent texts were very much better. The advent of the National Curriculum means that primary schools will have to invest in new geography materials, and these are likely to be written and researched with a much wider perspective than earlier materials. However, school and class libraries are still likely to contain dated material, much of which may be incorrect.

Fieldwork

Another source of difficulty for many girls is fieldwork. We live in a society which can be very dangerous. Girls are felt to be particularly at risk, and this makes formal and informal exploration of the environment difficult. Clothing is a related problem. Girls are often expected to wear to school clothing which is far from suitable for fieldwork, or even for a casual walk round the uncut areas of the school playing field. Shoes can be another source of difficulty; again, a glance at the type of footwear worn by even very young children can be an eye-opener. The ancient Chinese practice of footbinding may be incomprehensible to us, yet the sandals and heeled shoes worn by many infants can have a similar effect.

Even planned fieldwork can lead to problems when girls are expected to wear clothing in which they feel uncomfortable – for example, trousers and heavy boots. Also, fieldwork frequently involves getting engaged in 'unfeminine activities', like getting dirty and climbing over fences. This may lead some pupils to feel that geography is not for them.

History

The History Working Party has not been faced with particular gender issues related to attitude and performance in history. Their dilemma, which in fact has proved to be part of a very much wider issue, is that of content.

Historical content

The teaching of history within the National Curriculum has caused more controversy than any other subject. An earlier HMI document quoted the words of Khrushchev: 'Historians are dangerous people. They are capable of upsetting everything.' The teaching of history in schools is seen by many people as a powerful propaganda tool. Historical 'facts' are open to various interpretations, and the sheer quantity of material from the past means that facts have to be selected carefully. This is particularly true at primary level, since primary history texts are vulnerable to simplistic writing styles, generalisations and inaccuracies.

Those who argue for a skills-based approach to history do so partly in order to overcome a heavy reliance on this traditionally produced factual material. The introcuction of historical skills is seen as a means of providing pupils with the ability and interest necessary to come to terms with material from the past.

The History Working Party discussed this in great detail in their reports, but all the discussion has not altered the fact that there have been huge dilemmas about exactly what the content of the curriculum should be. Just before the delayed publication of the final report, the *Times Educational Supplement* asked several prominent personalities – historians and others – what they would include in their list of important facts that children should know. The result was as varied as might be expected. Historical content takes on important political implications, whatever the approach to teaching.

Gender, race and class issues are seen as part of the controversy about content. The Working Party acknowledged that many events in the past were '...recorded in terms of the 'heroic' deeds of men in battle etc, while both records and text-books fail to report adequately the role of women, so giving an unbalanced picture of the past'. (11.21)

This imbalance also extends in general to the areas of class and race. The report goes on:

'11.22 History shows that social arrangements need not and will not always remain as they are. It also shows that certain groups have been treated more or less favourably in some societies than in others.

11.23 Teachers should give careful thought to differences in the historical roles of men and women and draw attention to them wherever it is appropriate. We have shown in the programme of study some essential issues which affected men and women in different ways. Some teachers will want, and some pupils may urge, a more conscious and systematic approach to gender in their history classes. We recommend that, whatever weight is given to gender, it should be treated broadly, as one among many ways in which societies define and divide people. It is helpful to consider the implications of historical events for both men and women and to avoid token lip-service to the history of women.

11.24 Our approach is intended to combat inherited stereotypes. Women should be studied not only as part of the social history (where it is assumed that they "belong") but in contexts often treated as exclusively "male", such as politics, war, commerce, and science. In this process the evidence for women's activities, often plentiful, should be heeded. In attempting to redress imbalances of perception through history teaching, it is important that the selection and interpretation of sources and topics should not become contrived or unbalanced in new ways'.

As with the Geography Report, the work of the History Working Party illustrates how deeply gender issues are involved in the content of history teaching in the primary school. However, the report gives teachers very little specific guidance as to how the imbalances can be redressed.

Historical context

The history attainment targets acknowledge the importance of encouraging children to examine the nature of history. At one level, this enables them to develop their own perspectives on the discipline. At another, it develops wider critical faculties for analysing the written word, questioning not only what is written down, but why and how a piece of evidence has been assembled. The controversy surrounding the history report needs in some ways to be replicated in schools, so that pupils learn of different ways of interpreting the past. Gender issues can be an important starting point. One ancient history textbook informs its readers that: 'Men learned to roast whole animals on a spit, turning the carcass from time to time to cook it evenly. When they could grow wheat, they ground the ears into flour with stones and baked rough bread.' (Quoted in Donovan and Hughes *Putting Women Back into History*).

Pupils can then be shown how archaeological and anthropological evidence has revealed that women in the Stone Age would have been busy and adept in food gathering, childcare, leather work, making garments, slings and containers from animal skins, cooking, pottery, weaving grasses, reeds and bark strips for baskets, fashioning beads and ornaments from teeth or bone, constructing shelters, making tools for a variety of uses, and using plants and herbs for medicine. Each one of these is a topic in itself!

Humanities strategies

In primary geography and history, strategies for gender issues have concentrated on analysing and extending skills acquired both at home and at school. The possibilities for education in the humanities need to be seized early.

Nursery schools

Nurseries that encourage all the children to explore their immediate environment are well on the way to helping them develop a healthy curiosity about the physical world. This is particularly important for children who have poor play facilities, a factor which is not always related to the socio-economic statusof the family.

Play

Children's choices for outdoor play are often gender-related. Geographical skills, concepts and attitudes can be reinforced by encouraging children to ride tricycles and trundle cars, use larger climbing apparatus and so on. It is important that all children have the opportunity to gain these experiences, particularly those who may not have them out of school.

Clothing

Ensuring that children come into school suitably dressed depends on two factors.
• An awareness on the part of the child's carers about what is suitable. Good relationships between school and home can minimise problems in this area.
• An open attitude within the school about what may or may not be unsuitably restrictive clothing.

Many girls wear trousers at home, and there is much to be said for letting them do so at school, since trousers provide more freedom of movement than skirts and dresses. In this respect the clothing of some ethnic minority groups is far less restrictive than the traditional English school uniform, with tie and shirt for boys, and skirt for girls. Staff also need to be able to wear suitable clothing for school. Again, trousers may be far more suitable than skirts for most primary teachers. A surprising number of headteachers still insist that smart dress means a skirt or dress for female staff. This may be unnecessarily inhibiting for female teachers, who do after all provide important role models for both boys and girls.

Local geography

Monitoring for gender differences in knowledge of local geography can be done by asking children to draw and talk about what they do outside school. This has to be done with care and with knowledge about the children concerned. Ask questions, such as how far they are allowed to go alone or with a friend, what sorts of toys, games and puzzles they have, and where they visit with their families.

Information like this can be built up informally or by a systematic recording of children's own work. 'My journey to school' maps are another very easy way of recording, and provide interesting comparisons for children as they grow older. They also help children to become more geographically aware.

Local studies

There is a local context for much of the history and geography at primary level, particularly at Key Stage 1, and content will therefore have to include race, gender and class perspectives.

The history and geography of any local community involves all its citizens, and studying it can provide an opportunity for pupils to see women in roles other than those of parents and teachers.

Using children's fiction

The activity web below forms part of a project on history through storytelling, with the theme of 'Grannies'. It shows how a picture book, in this case *My Grandmother Has Black Hair* by Mary Hoffman (Methuen), can be used to discuss various issues in a historical context. The grandmother in this story is very different from the story-book grannies with their grey hair tied in a bun. There is no way *she* would be fooled by a wolf! The story provides a good opening to a project about what grannies did when they were young; this one worked in a circus. The attainment targets in the web are taken from the Draft Orders for History.

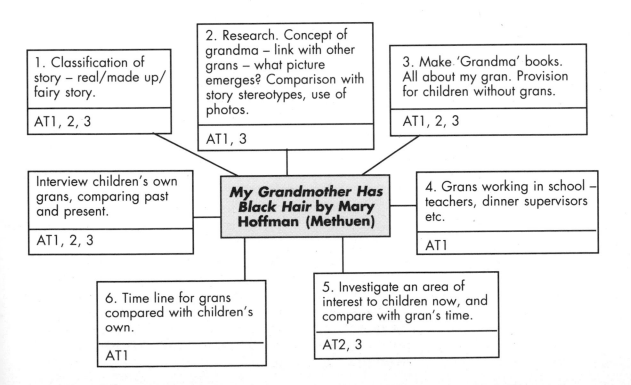

1. Classification of story – real/made up/ fairy story.

AT1, 2, 3

2. Research. Concept of grandma – link with other grans – what picture emerges? Comparison with story stereotypes, use of photos.

AT1, 3

3. Make 'Grandma' books. All about my gran. Provision for children without grans.

AT1, 2, 3

Interview children's own grans, comparing past and present.

AT1, 2, 3

My Grandmother Has Black Hair by Mary Hoffman (Methuen)

4. Grans working in school – teachers, dinner supervisors etc.

AT1

6. Time line for grans compared with children's own.

AT1

5. Investigate an area of interest to children now, and compare with gran's time.

AT2, 3

Assemblies

Recently produced books giving ideas for assemblies provide some very good stories about a wide range of people and places. Assembly is one way of sharing with a large number of people the experiences, feelings and thoughts of others.

Women's history weeks

Some LEAs and individual primary schools have held women's history weeks or fortnights, which bring people together to share resources. Library and museum services can also be involved, which helps to ensure a wider audience.

Wider horizons

For both geography and history, good resources become much scarcer as the context moves further away from the here and now. Few primary teachers want to be entirely dependent on published materials, but it would be naïve to expect all schools to produce their own schemes of work for every area of the curriculum. As both history and geography have often suffered from a lack of resourcing, teachers have frequently had to depend on gathering together their own materials. The following questions may help to ensure that these materials do not present stereotyped images.

• Does the word 'family' always assume a white nuclear family headed by a dad who works, a mum who stays at home and does the shopping, and two children?

• Is the concept of men's and women's work examined? There are ways in which differences in work expectations can be related to gender, race and class differences. These can be culturally based, and studied in human geography – for example, women farmers in Africa, who are expected to carry heavy loads and take responsibility for farming. Alternatively, they can be historically based – for example, changes in women's work over the years, such as domestic service and war work.

• Do books, videos, slides and posters reflect wider perspectives for the future as well as traditional patterns in the past?

• Is there proper provision for pupils to discuss these issues, so that they can begin to transfer skills and knowledge gained in the humanities to other areas of their lives?

TECHNOLOGY

Surprisingly little work has been done on gender issues in primary schools in relation to the design and technology element of the Technology report. Until quite recently, however, many aspects of design and technology were contained within the craft subjects, which were taught separately to girls and boys in many primary schools. Girls were taught needlework, while boys did craft.

These craft activities have been restructured more tightly in order to fit into a subject now called 'Technology'. Even the naming of this part of the curriculum has caused confusion and dissent. It started under the name of 'craft, design and technology', and then became known as 'design and technology', before finally emerging as 'technology'.

The whole issue of technology in secondary schools has had far more attention since the huge gender differences in the take-up of technical subjects became apparent. It is tempting once again to think that this is a secondary sector problem, but there are important issues here for primary schools. Many of the skills involved in technology are believed to be developed through socialisation patterns at home. Girls who help with domestic jobs such as cooking and cleaning learn specific skills from these activities, while boys who gain experience with DIY learn other skills. An Equal Opportunities Commission Working Party on craft, design and technology (CDT) felt that primary schools could provide compensatory play activities which might help develop skills of this sort in children who had missed them at home.

The Technology Final Orders should ensure that all pupils have a good grounding in technological skills. But the important question is to what extent experiences outside school can be built on and expanded in a non-stereotyped way for all pupils. Pupils who never watch or experience the use of particular tools outside school will feel less confident when called upon to use them in school. They will need plenty of practice with the equipment in order to acquire the skills which some of their peers will already have picked up at home. This applies as much to kitchen as as to garage equipment.

PHYSICAL EDUCATION

Physical education (PE) is the one area of the curriculum which is still openly gender-differentiated in many schools. At the time of writing the Working Party has not reported, but it is likely that this will be an issue upon which it will have to comment. PE also differs from other subjects in that many pupils spend a large amount of their free time involved in it. Sport has a high status for many pupils, and there is considerable evidence that ability at sports affects children's popularity. Not to be good at sport can therefore be a very traumatic experience for a boy, one which may seem much worse than failure in other areas of the curriculum.

Performance and attitudes

In the past, few researchers have looked at gender issues in relation to sport at primary level. It tended to be seen as a matter for secondary and post-school study, since by then the gender differences were blatantly obvious. However, it would be unprofessional for primary teachers not to examine gender issues in relation to PE in the primary school. By the time pupils are eleven, they have had at least seven years' experience of school-based physical education, and they are likely to draw on this experience when they encounter PE in the secondary school.

A report on secondary school PE by the Schools Council, published in 1984, also looked at pre-school and primary PE and games. Differences in physical movement were found, even at pre-school level, and boys and girls could be observed using their bodies differently in carrying out the same physical tasks. One example the report cited was throwing, where boys tended to put their whole bodies into motion, whereas girls concentrated, for the most part, on moving their arms. Teachers reported that boys enjoyed playing rough games in large groups, while girls preferred quieter activities in small groups.

Other studies confirm that boys play outdoors more than girls, that they play in larger groups, that they play more competitively and with a greater age mix in the groups. Differences have also been noted in relation to dance, where pupils use their imaginations and bodies differently – girls flowing and gyrating, boys moving in strong, powerful, machine-like ways. The Middle Schools survey noted that as boys grew older they tended to opt out of dance, and many girls' interest in PE decreased with age. This declining interest in PE by many girls has in the past been linked with the idea of sport as a 'macho' preoccupation. This trend continues in later life, since far fewer women take part in sport as a leisure or health activity than men.

The Schools Council project also noted the higher status awarded to boys' games, particularly football, and felt this influenced primary PE in many different ways, notably in the amount of time and resources spent on football. A study in Norfolk also noted the high status given to football and the difficulty that girls had at that time (in the early 1980s) if they wanted to play football.

Biological, social and cultural perspectives

Many people have deep convictions about women being unsuited to particular sporting activities because of biological limitations. This view is so pervasive that it often lies below the conscious level at which critical discussion can take place.

An ILEA study group for PE examined several biological explanations for differences in performance, including gender-based differences in strength, endurance and susceptibility to injury. They produced considerable evidence to show that women can participate in strenuous activity under all the conditions in which men participate. They also concluded that women were not in any way fulfilling their potential for sports. They pointed out that obstetrical and gynaecological data refuted the idea that severe exercise was the cause of undesirable effects. The study group concluded that physical endurance is no more damaging or overtaxing for women than it is for men.

There is considerable evidence that social and cultural factors have more bearing than physical differences upon gender-based variations in performance and attitude at primary school age. Several researches have shown that parental attitudes to children's play tend to be gender-differentiated. Boys are often allowed more freedom to explore the play environment, to display aggressive behaviour, and to engage in vigorous activities with toys.

The ILEA study showed that fathers wrestled more with sons and were more likely to teach them gross motor skills such as jumping and throwing than precise, delicate movements such as those involved in knot-tying. As children grow older, they tend to play with children of the same sex. This in turn may result in greater gender differentiation of play skills, since opposite-sex children may be excluded or discouraged from single-sex groups.

Strategies

Schools need a clear set of aims and objectives for their PE programmes. The Final Orders for the National Curriculum in PE are likely to be less prescriptive than in other subjects, so guidelines and policy statements will need more attention at school level.

Widening experiences

The whole range of movement should be experienced by all children, and the PE curriculum should provide them with the opportunity to develop physical skills which will be useful for a number of different games and sports. There is little difference in physical strength or muscle and fat distribution between boys and girls at primary age. In fact, there are likely to be as many differences between members of the same sex as there are between the sexes.

Mixed-sex PE

Many primary schools now have a policy of mixed-sex sport. At first, however, it may be necessary for some children to be taught certain skills in special groups.

Extending opportunities

Stereotyped images about sport need to be examined, and sport promoted as a worthwhile leisure activity. Many sports centres and clubs run after-school and holiday activities for children. Good centres have a wide variety of such activities, which can give children a chance to extend their sports repertoire as well as helping them to keep fit. Girls-only sessions have been put on by many LEAs as a form of positive discrimination (the 'special escalator') to encourage girls to use the facilities at other times.

Non-competitive sports

All children can succeed in co-operative games, and the same physical skills are put into practice by everyone –

often at exactly the same time, as for example in using a games parachute. Schools which do not want to take up non-competitive sports as an overall policy may nevertheless find many of the co-operative games and activities useful.

Multicultural sports

It can be very interesting to experiment with sports and games from a variety of cultures, but consideration has to be given to religious and cultural practices so that girls can participate fully.

Team games

Well-run team sports are enjoyable for the co-operation and team spirit they encourage. Pupils who do not excel at team sports are more likely to continue with individual sports in adulthood, so pupils need to have an opportunity to take part in both. There is considerable evidence to show that women are more likely to continue with individual sports than team sports.

Language

Words should be used carefully. Praising a girl because she 'runs like a boy' is not the best way of encouraging either her or other girls to exert themselves. Using language like this will give messages of power and status to devalue one sex in comparison with another, as when a boy is told he 'throws like a girl'.

Sports personalities

Role models are important. There are many good examples to cite at national and international level – male and female, black and white. Many local sports personalities are keen to encourage youngsters to take part in their sport and can provide a positive example right there in the classroom. This also provides a chance for children to widen their knowledge of locally available sports activities. A constant diet of sport on television can narrow their perspectives.

Resources

The different status of male and female sports and, consequently, the resources allocated to them may need careful examination in some schools.

Use of space

Domination of playground space by one particular group should be avoided. A group of boys using most of the available space for a game of football may be pushing girls and non-football-playing boys aside, and, apart from anything else, it is just unfair. It teaches subservience and aggression, as well as limiting the activities of all those who play outside – including the footballers. Some schools limit large balls to one area of a large playground. Schools with smaller play areas have banned large balls altogether.

The whole question of the hidden curriculum of playgrounds is raised in the next chapter, and some strategies are suggested there.

MUSIC

For many primary pupils, music is what they hear on the radio or when watching videos and television. Their musical education at primary school will vary a great deal, depending on their school's practice and/or the capability of their teacher. Some children may gain extra musical experiences through their LEA musical teams, and some may have lessons privately. At this stage it is difficult to know what difference the National Curriculum will make, but there is evidence that the centrally-based LEA music teams are being 'rationalised' as a result of the Education Reform Act.

Monitoring gender issues in this area of the curriculum raises similar issues to those revealed elsewhere. The limited data available at secondary level has shown that girls are more likely to have positive attitudes to music than boys, with a better record for performance and listening, and a higher success rate at all examinations in the subject. However, there are still more male than female professional instrumentalists.

Organising the curriculum

A clear policy statement should set out the aims, objectives and expected outcomes for music within the school. It should also provide a broad international perspective.

A good music curriculum should involve listening, performing and composing. All these activities are essential for a full musical education. However, not all teachers feel competent in music, and some schools have no one to lead this part of the curriculum. A school statement should recognise the musical competence of existing staff.

Choosing activities

Staff need to be sure that they are not excluding particular musical activities because they are disliked by boys or girls. The musical tasks must be varied enough to enable boys and girls to contribute, and teachers also need to allocate other classroom tasks fairly. Are the activities organised by rota, by pupil preference or by direction from the teacher? For example:

- allocation of popular instruments;
- getting instruments in and out of cupboards;
- helping with class management, arranging furniture, etc.

There is much to be said for having a rota, which can be seen to be fair. Older children can draw this up themselves.

Music outside school .

Children's musical experiences out of school need examining. The lyrics of many popular songs raise important issues about relationships and feelings, and may suggest a way to discuss emotion and imagination in relation to musical activities. Obviously, careful choices have to be made!

Assessing resources

As with other areas of the curriculum, pupils can pick up important messages about music from the books and posters they see both inside and outside school. Pictures are more likely to show a man as a conductor, sound engineer, disc jockey, composer, record producer or soloist. Women are more likely to be shown as singers, accompanists, music teachers or as part of an audience. Children can be asked to find pictures of men and women playing different instruments.

ART

In the west, white male artists have traditionally been seen as the norm. This not only excludes black people and white women, but also exemplifies a western inability to take seriously the work of people from other cultures. Redressing this imbalance should not simply involve 'adding on' the work of women as some form of optional extra. Examining art from a wider perspective involves challenging our preconceptions.

One way of doing this is to examine the categories that make up what we think of as art, and to explore how gender operates within them.

Challenging stereotypes

Ask children to draw an artist. This request generally results in pictures of white men with paint brushes and easels. Stereotypes like this can be challenged with some of the beautiful illustrations by women in children's picture books. Even very young children can learn to recognise the work of artists who are particular favourites.

Assessing images

The portrayal of women as sex objects occurs in various ways in the primary curriculum – usually unintentionally. As a fairly mature (but inexperienced) student on teaching practice, I once asked children to bring in newspapers for an art lesson, only to be faced with a sea of 'page threes'. We had a discussion about why photographs like this were shown in newspapers, but experience taught me to use newspapers from home next time we had such a lesson! Some teachers have had children writing to newspapers to complain about 'page three' pictures. It is not only women who find them objectionable; men may also object to the assumption that they want their newspapers to contain such images.

A study of the visual images of women, men and children used in advertising can be another way of tackling the issue. Collage work on this subject provides its own messages, with little help from teachers. The colours used to surround 'feminine' products – pastel shades, pinks and light yellows – can be compared with the 'macho' images of boys and young men. An element of humour has crept into some advertisements in relation to sex stereotyping, and this can make the whole issue much less heavy.

'Women's' arts

Children's early pictures may be used to start discussions about how they see the roles of men and women. Careful discussion often produces non-traditional responses, as traditional family networks operate differently under changed circumstances, and many children do not come from a traditional nuclear family.

The traditional arts undertaken by women in the west, such as quilt-making and embroidery, need to be given as much status as those undertaken by men, such as painting and sculpture. Margaret Mead once wrote that, 'If men took to knitting it would become an art' (Male and Female, 1949). Kaffe Fasset did just that and proved her right.

RESOURCES

Humanities

Geography

Blyth, A. (1990) *Making the Grade for Primary Humanities* (Open University Press).

Geography Working Party (1990) *Geography for ages 5 to 16* (HMSO).

HMI (1988) *Aspects of the Teaching and Learning of History and Geography* (HMSO).

Matthews, D.H. (1986) 'Gender, Graphicacy and Geography', in *Educational Review*, Vol. 38, No. 3.

Women and Geography Study Group of the IBG (1984) *Geography and Gender* (Hutchinson).

History

Cox, K. and Hughes, P. (1990) *Early Years History, An Approach Through Story* (LIHE).

DES (1990) *History for ages 5 to 16* (DES).

Durbin, G. Morris, S. and Wilkinson, S. (1990) *Learning from Objects* (English Heritage).

Ealing Gender Equality Team (1988) *Write Women Back into History: Reports from Teachers* (Ealing Education Service).

Fryer, P. (1985) *Staying Power: The History of Black People in Britain* (Pluto Press).

History Working Group (1990) *Final Report* (HMSO).

Hoffman, M. and Burroughes, J. (1988) *My Grandma has Black Hair* (Methuen).

Morris, S. (1989) *Using Portraits* (English Heritage).

Welbourne, D. (1990) 'Deconstruction to Reconstruction: An Approach to Women's History through Local History' in *Teaching History* (April).

Local history

Local Records Offices have records which include information on local issues. The records may need to be used critically, as those who kept them may not have been sympathetic with the issues involved. Possible sources of information include the following:

Census Returns – information on occupations, family and household size and age structure.

Parish Registers – baptisms, marriages, burials, occupations and age of those married. Levels of literacy are attested by use of crosses instead of signatures.

Trade Directories – information on women in shops and businesses.

School Log Books – show reasons for absences.
Photographs – family life, street life, shops, work, rural conditions.
Poor Law overseers accounts and **workhouse minutes** – information on relief given.

Museums and galleries also offer useful background information, materials and talks for school groups. Trips to art galleries and collections of postcards of portraits can provide useful information about the past.

Technology

Harrison, P. and Ryan, C. (1990/1) Technology in Action Units 1-5 (Folens).

PE

Deem, R. (1984) *Women and Leisure* (Open University Press).
ILEA (1984) *Providing Equal Opportunities for Girls and Boys in Physical Education* (ILEA).
Leoman, O. (1984) *'Sit on the sidelines and watch the boys play': Sex differentiation in physical education* (Longman).
May, N. and Ruddock, J. (1983) *Sex Stereotyping and the Early Years of Schooling* (University of East Anglia).
Scraton, S. (1986) 'Gender and Girls' Physical Education' in *British Journal of Physical Education*, Vol. 17, no.4.
Wetton, P. (1990) 'Give Girls a Chance' in *Child Education* (February).

Co-operative games

Masheder, M. (1986) *Let's Co-operate* (Peace Pledge Union).
Masheder, M. (1989) *Let's Play Together : Co-operative games for all ages* (Green Pink).
Orlick, T. (1982) *The Second Co-operative Sports and Games Book* (Pantheon Books).
Pax Christi (1980) *Winners All* (Pax Christi, 9 Henry Road, London N4 2LH).

Music

ILEA (1985) *Primary Matters* (ILEA).
Wills, G. (1987) 'Music' in *'Genderwatch!'* (SCDC).

Art

Brent LEA (1985) *Steps to Equality* (Brent LEA).
Connolly, J. and Garb, T. (1987) 'Art' in *Genderwatch* (SCDC).
Mead, Margaret (1949) *Male and Female* (Dell).

7 PERSONAL AND SOCIAL EDUCATION

Children do not learn only from formal lessons; they also learn much that is unplanned. This unplanned element of schooling was not catered for in the original consultative document on the National Curriculum.

Cross-curricular issues can provide a framework within which to structure the total activity of a school. As the National Curriculum Council's Circular 6 states, the cross-curricular dimensions are concerned with the 'intentional promotion of personal and social development through the curriculum as a whole'.

Personal and social education (PSE) is a fairly recent addition to the formal primary school agenda. Before the National Curriculum it was seen as an attempt to consider explicitly what primary teachers have always agreed is an essential part of their role – the personal, social and moral development of children. This idea is often vaguely presented in a school's statement of aims as a wish to help each child realise his or her potential. In tackling this issue, PSE is also attempting to pick up and codify some elements of what has been termed the 'hidden curriculum'.

As already mentioned, the hidden curriculum is by its very nature difficult to pin down. However, it is through the hidden curriculum that messages are transmitted to the children and to others working in the school about the status and character of both individuals and social groups. The hidden curriculum operates through the rules, rituals and routines of the school. It operates through attitudes and through omissions – what we do *not* teach is often more influential than what we do teach.

Making personal and social objectives explicit within the work of the school does not necessarily mean giving them a specific time allocation. Many secondary schools attempt to cover the objectives of PSE by making it a timetabled subject, with lessons covering topics as various as income tax, AIDS, gender and race issues. In a primary school, however, much of what is required can be carried out through the day-to-day relationships and activities which form a normal part of the school's organisation. The growing recognition of the need to examine implicit values at work in schools has greatly increased the importance given to PSE as an identifiable aspect of the primary curriculum.

Gender issues inevitably form part of PSE, as confirmed by Circular 6. The circular also recognises that in primary schools important cross-curricular dimensions such as equal opportunities and multicultural education will not necessarily be delivered through specific courses of PSE, as they may be in the secondary school. *The Whole Curriculum*, which forms part of the National Curriculum Council's series on curriculum guidance, provides a very broad definition of PSE:

'The cross-curricular elements so far described are significant but do not encompass all that is PSE. The themes are concerned with the physical, sexual, moral, social and vocational self, but subjects of the National Curriculum, religious education, additional subjects and the extra-curricular activities described in this guidance also play their part. How the curriculum is managed, its organisation and the teaching methods deployed; the unique combination of factors which create the ethos of a school – its aims, attitudes, values and procedures – all make an important contribution to personal and social education programmes in school.

'The education system is charged with preparing young people to take their place in a wide range of roles in adult life. It also has a duty to educate the individuals to be able to think and act for themselves, with an acceptable set of personal qualities and values which also meet the wider social demands of adult life. In short the personal and social development of pupils is a major aim of education; personal and social education being the means by which this aim is achieved.'

GENDER AS PART OF A PSE PROGRAMME

The web below shows one way in which gender issues can fit into a PSE programme.

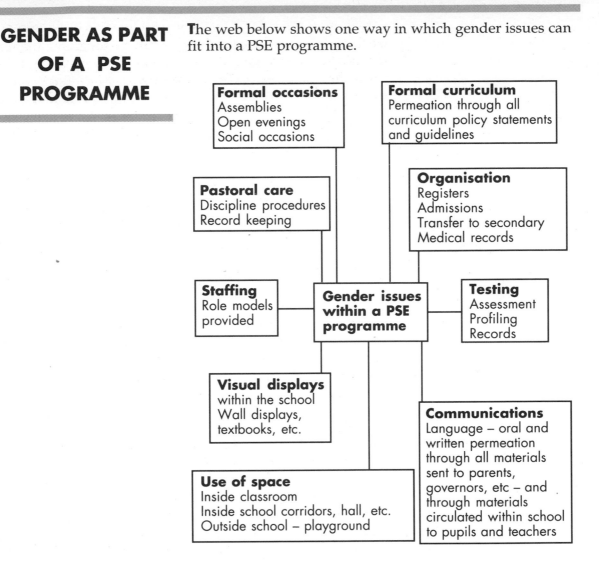

Formal occasions
Assemblies
Open evenings
Social occasions

Formal curriculum
Permeation through all curriculum policy statements and guidelines

Pastoral care
Discipline procedures
Record keeping

Organisation
Registers
Admissions
Transfer to secondary
Medical records

Staffing
Role models provided

Gender issues within a PSE programme

Testing
Assessment
Profiling
Records

Visual displays
within the school
Wall displays,
textbooks, etc.

Communications
Language – oral and written permeation through all materials sent to parents, governors, etc – and through materials circulated within school to pupils and teachers

Use of space
Inside classroom
Inside school corridors, hall, etc.
Outside school – playground

Peter Lang, in his book *Thinking About Personal and Social Education in the Primary School*, gives a useful preliminary discussion list which can be used to highlight areas of a PSE programme where gender issues may be significant. The degree of significance will depend on how a school identifies its intended outcomes for a PSE programme and on the teachers' own awareness of gender issues.

Peter Lang's list of hoped-for outcomes for PSE includes the following points:

'•mutual trust between child and child, child and teacher, teacher and teacher, teacher and parents;
• children regarding themselves and others as persons of

value whatever their sex, colour, creed or appearance;
• children confident in relation to staff, parents, visitors, adults (welcome and unwelcome);
• children more interested in learning and better learners as a result of being regarded as persons rather than vessels for learning;
• children more able to cope with conflict, crises and transitions, success and failure, pain and joy etc;
• children having responsible attitudes to themselves and others and to their learning in and out of school;
• children understanding and relating to the groups of which they are part and becoming aware of the communities and societies of which these groups are part.'

Children's view of themselves in all these areas will be influenced, positively or negatively, by their gender identity. Any school should aim to ensure that children have a wide range of non-stereotyped behaviour and attitudes from which to make decisions and choices.

The identification of gender issues within the hidden curriculum has already been covered, in part, in examining the core and foundation subjects. Awareness of gender issues can be identified through:
• curriculum policy statements and guidelines;
• the language used in school literature such as curriculum statements, the school prospectus, discipline policy, equal opportunities policy, the School Development Plan (SDP), job descriptions, worksheets, letters to parents and reports;
• the language used in visual displays within the school, both on its walls and in its teaching materials.

A key element in any PSE programme must be the relationships between the different individuals working within the school. An examination of the relationships between teacher and pupils, and between the pupils themselves, involves looking at teacher and pupil behaviour and at formal school routines.

PUPIL AND TEACHER RELATIONSHIPS

Teacher attitudes and expectations

Teachers' attitudes towards their pupils, the language that they use and the sorts of interactions they have with their pupils are important aspects of any child's experience of school. If teacher behaviour is influenced by gender-related issues, this will form an important part of children's perceptions about what it is to be a boy or girl in school.

This is an area of great complexity. It is scarcely surprising, therefore, that relatively little work has been done either on teacher expectations of children in primary school or on the effects that these expectations may have on the children concerned.

The central proposition in studies of teacher expectations is that pupils tend to perform as well or as badly as their teachers expect. This is a fairly simplistic view, and almost impossible to prove. It may be more helpful to suggest that the interaction between teachers and pupils is bound to be a powerful determinant of a pupil's self-image and confidence, particularly at primary level.

Researchers in the field of gender differentiation have also questioned whether teacher expectations of gender-related behaviour by pupils have affected pupils' views of themselves and their academic progress. Since there has been no widespread survey on teacher expectations in primary schools, this may be an area for the individual teacher/researcher to take up. Teachers who have done this have found some general patterns, which may sometimes be conflicting.

• Teachers value female and male pupils equally, but describe their typical behaviour as being different.

• Adjectives used to describe boys include non-compliant, demanding, excitable, talkative, attention-seeking and active.

• Girls tend to be described as gentler, more caring, sensible, obedient, hardworking, co-operative, quiet, dependent and passive.

• Boys and girls who diverge from these stereotypes by a considerable degree are likely to be labelled as deviant – a real sissy, mummy's boy (about boys), hard-faced, a real madam (about girls).

This sort of labelling produces a particularly difficult situation for boys. Girls' 'deviant' or 'boy-like' behaviour can be put down to the child being a 'tomboy'. This is a recognised pattern of development, which children grow out of. There are enough tomboys in fiction and on the television to reassure girls that their behaviour is quite normal; fictional examples are George in Enid Blyton's *Famous Five* stories and Jo in *Little Women*.

'Deviant' or 'girl-like' behaviour in boys meets with a different response. There is no name as positive as 'tomboy' for a boy who acts out of role. The negative nouns and adjectives abound – 'sissy', 'wimp', 'pansy' and so on.

Some picture books, for example Antony Browne's *Willy the Wimp* and Tomie de Paola's *Oliver Button is a sissy*, do explore these issues. Although these are aimed at young children, it is possible to use them with older children to discuss such issues 'at a distance'. Many older boys find this is far less threatening, although success is heavily dependent on the relationship the teacher has built up with the class.

Because the behaviour of boys and girls is perceived to be different, they tend to be treated differently:

• boys receive greater interaction from teachers for approval, disapproval and instruction;

• girls receive less attention, but are criticised more for their lack of knowledge and skill than for bad behaviour.

We move rapidly into the realms of speculation when we try to decide what effect this has on individual children. Some teachers have suggested that because girls get less attention they have lower self-esteem, but this does not fit with the observation that boys are more likely to be criticised for their behaviour. The idea that girls mature earlier may result in their being given more reponsibilities and less attention, but it may also result in an expectation that their learning patterns will slow down while those of boys will increase.

We cannot ignore the gender experiences that teachers bring into school with them. They are role models for children and, for many very young children, teachers are their first adult role models other than their parents. Our own experiences are bound to influence how we see boys and girls, both now and in the future. An awareness of this is an important first move towards ensuring a more equitable treatment of boys and girls within the classroom.

Exploration of these issues in small primary schools can be difficult when individual members of staff have widely differing views. Survival in the staff room is frequently achieved by consensus, and by acknowledging that some issues should not be discussed. However, gender issues, like other dimensions within the National Curriculum, need exploring as part of professional development. It is the personal nature of the subject that makes discussion about equal opportunities one of the most difficult aspects of the primary curriculum. Persuading the very traditional teacher that gender roles are changing and that schools need to acknowledge and prepare children for this is difficult and time-consuming.

The ideas that follow have been used at various times with different groups of primary teachers, men and women. They aim to enable teachers to examine their own views about what it means to be a man or woman. Some teachers may not want to disclose this to their colleagues, and their privacy should be respected.

Good things and bad things

Ask the teachers to write down individually or in pairs:
• some good things about being a man;
• some good things about being a woman;
• the disadvantages of being a man;
• the disadvantages of being a woman.
They can then share their findings.

A less threatening way of doing this is to ask colleagues to get the children themselves to make the lists, and then discuss the findings and work out the implications. Early years teachers can do this as part of a group or class discussion. Differences in opinions between children in different classes may indicate age differences or a difference in the messages being conveyed by class teachers. Such differences are likely to be more distinct at primary than at secondary level.

Discussing examples

Ask staff prior to in-service training to think of two high achievers in their class and two low achievers. Ask them to describe the children's qualities and consider how far their own expectations of these children are affected by gender, race and class.

Self-esteem

Much is made of the importance of building up children's self-esteem, but there is just as strong a need to do likewise for teachers. An indirect way of examining how people see themselves is to ask how they became teachers. The answers can be surprising. On one occasion, a teacher told us that she had received no careers advice at all, except that she should not wear black patent leather shoes, as they would reflect her underwear! She became a nursery teacher.

Differences in the advice given to male and female teachers can provide a good opportunity to discuss some of the very real difficulties for men wanting to teach young children, and the assumption that they will want to leave the classroom as soon as possible to become senior managers. Older men who have stayed as class teachers are frequently seen and treated as failures, on the assumption that they would be headteachers if they were any good.

Verbal interaction

This is one of the most controversial areas in which to ask teachers to examine their own practice, since it impinges on the belief that we treat all children in the same way. There is, however, considerable research evidence to indicate that we do not. Even if only to falsify this evidence, it is useful for teachers to re-examine the sorts of verbal interactions that go on in their classrooms. A checklist has been devised to do this (see Chapter Three, page 55), and other ideas for classroom monitoring are also given in Chapter Three.

Primary teachers have to cope with approximately 1000 verbal exchanges between themselves and their pupils in any one day. The vast majority of these are initiated by the teacher, and teacher-pupil conversations can form up to 80 per cent of the total talk within a classroom. Several American-based studies on elementary pupils have shown, however, that boys receive a greater percentage of teacher-pupil interchanges than girls, whether instructional, managerial or prohibitory. The Oracle survey in the UK also found that boys received more individual attention than girls, although they felt this was partly because boys were more likely to be low achievers, and teachers gave this group more attention.

Work in Cleveland nurseries (see Chapter Three, pages 52 to 53) found that boys and girls received approximately the same amount of adult-initiated talk, but that there were considerable differences in the type of interaction. Adults offered more help to girls than to boys, they questioned girls' intentions more and chatted socially more to them. They elaborated the play of boys more and gave them more information. As in other studies, it was found that adults managed and directed the behaviour of boys more.

It is difficult to know exactly how to interpret these findings. If boys are more disruptive, teachers will have to spend more time managing and directing their behaviour. On the other hand, if teachers expect boys to be more disruptive, they may sometimes be creating the behaviour to which they then have to respond. No one said dealing with this problem was going to be easy, but a heightened awareness of the issues may enable responses to be more professionally directed. As Chapter Three suggests, discussing the issues with the children themselves is one way of involving all pupils in formulating the rules and routines for classroom behaviour.

Classroom management

The ways primary school teachers organise their classrooms will reflect their attitudes to and expectations of pupils' behaviour and learning. This, in turn, may reinforce their preconceived ideas about particular sorts of behaviour. For many class teachers, good classroom management is seen in terms of efficient classroom organisation and control. This emphasis is reflected in initial teacher training, and students are advised that these are distinct areas in which their performance will be judged. An examination of many classrooms indicates that some teachers use gender differentiation as a key management technique.

Jobs

Jobs may be organised in a gender-differentiated way, with boys moving furniture, girls tidying up. This creates a climate in which children learn sex roles. If girls always wash paint pots and boys always put away the chairs, it is scarcely surprising if, by the time they reach the final year of the primary school, the girls are better at tidying up and the boys are better at stacking chairs. Gender differentiation gives children two messages. Firstly, they learn that boys do one job, girls another; and secondly, they actually learn how to become skilled in one activity (i.e. moving chairs) but not in another (i.e. sweeping up).

For the class teacher, an easy solution to the problem of jobs is to have an alphabetical list of all the children, and move down this in order, allocating jobs in turn. This has the added advantage of being seen to be fair by the children themselves. Primary teachers who do not have their own class need to work closely with individual class teachers, or devise their own rota system. Children soon spot a 'favourite', and a jobs rota is a simple way of cutting this out.

Headteachers are often in a particularly invidious position. One school avoids this problem by having two fourth-year pupils sitting and working in the foyer on a rota system. These two are responsible for welcoming all visitors to the school, showing them around if necessary, answering the phone and generally acting as a liaison for the many interactions between the outside world and the school.

Lining up

Children at school are often asked to line up. At one time, this was done automatically by forming one line of boys and one line of girls. Some teachers still argue that this is the only way of lining up. Others point out that it touches on a key equal opportunities issue and that, just as we would not dream of lining black and white pupils up separately, we should not be doing this with boys and girls.

There are numerous ways in which a class can line up and move around the school in safety. Pupils themselves can devise ways in which this can be done – by month of birth, position in the classroom, height, forename (A-H in one line, I-Z in the other), surname, or colour of clothing (impossible with uniform!). Some important mathematical points can be made at the same time concerning sets, such as that if we have only two lines, we have to be careful that the classifications do not overlap.

Control

The level of noise within a classroom is still seen as an important criterion for classroom management. This is scarcely surprising if one teacher is responsible for 30 or more pupils. A noisy classroom is difficult for anyone to work in. However, assessments of the difference between a 'good working atmosphere' and a 'noisy' one are necessarily subjective. Teachers' own feelings will vary, depending on the nature of the activity and how they feel about it.

There is some agreement about what constitutes unacceptable noise. Children learn this early in their lives, just as they learn that noise is a great attention winner. A parent may be able to leave a noisy child for a while, but a teacher cannot. Several researchers have noted that girls who withdraw quietly from a lesson often get away with it because they are not making a noise. Boys' withdrawal tends to be noisier and causes the teacher to take action. Disruptive boys can dominate a classroom and ultimately have lessons geared to their interests. Girls who opt out may be forgotten.

Awareness of the issue is an important first step to dealing with this problem, particularly if the school operates a topic-based approach to its curriculum. Topics needed to be broadly based, and should enable all pupils to enjoy, contribute and learn. The issues involved should be discussed within individual classrooms, as all pupils can suffer from the behaviour of a few. One of the side effects of Standard Assessment Tasks is likely to be that seriously disruptive pupils are even less likely to stay within mainstream education. As the statistics on page 37 show, disruptive pupils are far more likely to be boys than girls.

Seating and grouping arrangements

Teachers have a variety of ways in which they can group children. The most common are based on:
• friendship – where the teacher lets the children decide where they wish to sit;
• ability – generally according to reading ability and powers of concentration;
• gender – boy/girl, boy/girl, 'so they don't talk so much!'
Differences in the perceived purposes of education determine to some extent how teachers group children. The practice of punishing a child by sitting him or her next to someone of the opposite sex creates a dangerous precedent. There is an implication that boys and girls should not get on with each other; in the long run this causes far more problems in classroom managment than it solves.

General organisation

There is likely to be a whole-school policy relating to the organisation of registers, class lists, filing systems, record cards and the like. The argument for the gender-differentiation of these records is that it is a requirement of DES Form 7 returns. There is little that the class teacher can do about this, as the final decision lies with the headteacher and/or LEA. However, as more and more schools use computer-based administrative systems, they will have more opportunity to experiment with their own methods. Many schools without the advantage of computer data bases also have all their administration done alphabetically. They argue that children learn much from being divided up like this and it minimises the sense of the differences between children.

Assemblies

Organisation

Assemblies give an opportunity for a formal display of the school's ethos. For an outsider, they provide a fascinating insight into the values of the school. If we consider only the non-religious aspects, there are various questions that can be posed, the answers to which can give clues to the hidden messages primary school pupils are receiving about the purposes of assemblies and of school life generally.
• Do staff attend, or are assemblies a way of providing precious non-contact time?
• How involved are the pupils in the overall presentation of assemblies?
• Who takes the assembly – the head, the deputy, or class teachers?
• How often does it take place – daily, three times a week, infrequently?
• Is the format always the same?
• Do people from the community come in as listeners, as speakers, or both?
  Gender issues are significant here if the following conditions apply:
• if assemblies are always presented by a member of one sex – for example, a male headteacher;
• if pupil readers are generally of one sex;
• if badly-behaved pupils who disrupt proceedings are generally boys;
• if those coming in from the community represent stereotyped roles or make presentations which are overtly sexist;
• if some events and activities receive a disproportionate amount of time and praise in comparison to others – for example, the achievements of the boys' football team as compared to those of the girls' netball team.

Content

There are some excellent resources for assemblies (see the resource list at the end of this chapter) which contain a wide range of non-sexist and multicultural material in addition to the more traditional fare. Much of the language and symbolism involved in assemblies is far more complicated than adults seem to realise, and it is useful to make explicit the routine parts of any form of ritual, particularly if it can be interpreted as sexist.

TEACHERS AND PARENTS

Communication

The class teacher is often the front-line communicator with the children's parents and carers. Communication involves:
• sending written messages home;
• sending oral messages home;
• having parents in as helpers;
• discussing children's progress, academic and social;
• acting as a social worker for parents who may see no other adult whom they can trust.

The way the communications are handled can provide powerful messages to children.
• If written messages are always addressed to Mr and Mrs (child's surname), this assumes a particular family set up, which for many children just does not exist. Knowledge of naming structures in other cultures is also essential.
• It is often assumed that the receiver of messages will be the child's mother – 'Give mummy the note', 'Ask your mother to come in and see me'. Many male carers want to be involved in their child's school life, and we certainly should be trying to involve those who are less responsible.

Helpers in school

The overwhelming majority of helpers in primary schools are women, even in areas of high male unemployment and where shift work means that men are available during the daytime. Individual schools need first to examine the sorts of messages that this provides for children:
• about women, if only women help;
• about men, if only women help;
• if their own parent(s) or carers are unable to help.

Secondly, schools need to consider how to encourage more men into school, particularly into non-stereotyped areas. Schools can:
• encourage the presence of more male primary school teachers, particularly in the early years;

• involve men in the organisation of parental support units, or their equivalent.

• provide a clear statement that both male and female carers are valued.

BEHAVIOUR BETWEEN PUPILS

General interaction

When children first enter the nursery at around three years of age, there is usually a considerable degree of friendship and play across the genders. This can last well into infant school, but by the age of four or five children generally seem to be growing more aware of their own gender identity. As children get older, they tend to interact and play more with children of their own sex. This has important consequences, which are recognised by most teachers.

• Peer interactions may exclude each sex from the other's games, interests and play areas, so that initial differences between the sexes in particular activities may become exaggerated.

• Different power and status groupings develop. These are frequently based on gender and race. Evidence for this can be found in name-calling and in the domination of play spaces. As the interaction between these two ten-year-olds indicates, children themselves recognise the effects of such domination.

'Jessica: But the boys think they kinda rule the football pitch. You can't often play football. You might be able to play but you'd be lucky if you would. Normally it's just the boys on the football pitch.

Mary: We have to play in the middle and outside the football pitch. Sometimes we play down the side. Sometimes we don't play anything. We sit by the sides and talk about things...'

(Weiner, *Just a Bunch of Girls*.)

Primary teachers are usually in a position to control much of the interaction between pupils inside school, if they recognise what is going on. Domination of space takes place within classrooms. Examples include:

• pushing others aside;

• seizing and misusing materials (often personal possessions);

• rocking on chairs;

• stretching over and having an additional turn with a scarce resource, such as a computer.

A set of clearly defined rules and routines, preferably drawn up by the children themselves, allows pupils to recognise their own behaviour patterns as well as that of others.

Some of the worst problems in the relationships between pupils occur outside school, before and after school, at playtimes and lunchtimes.

The playground

Playground issues affect everyone. The playground is also one of the most public places in a school, where children, teachers and other adults can be seen together. Children playing in the playground are visible to a wide variety of people, both those within the school itself and those passing by outside. Problems and questions which arise from the ways in which children behave in the playground affect many different groups of people:
• parents bringing children to and from school;
• parents working in school;
• the headteacher and other teachers;
• other pupils in school;
• pupils at other schools, including former pupils;
• other members of the community who pass or enter the school, including governors;
• lunch-time supervisors.

Parents

In some schools, playground-related incidents are the main reason for informal visits of parents to school. There are several reasons for this.
• Children are afraid – of fighting, bullying, name calling, having no one to play with, sexual harassment (boys pulling up girls' skirts, running in and out of the girls' toilets, etc.).
• Parents are afraid for their children – because of a lack of adult supervision, a lack of structure to activities, the weather in which children are expected to play outside, and many other factors.
• Parents are concerned about aspects of the hidden curriculum - their children learning bad language, learning to fight to defend themselves, having to win friends with sweets, etc.

Children

Children themselves voice concern about playtimes. Most teachers are familiar with the 'Please, can I stay in and tidy up for you?' syndrome, as well as with the child who goes out and is immediately sent back inside for misbehaviour.

Teachers

Teachers frequently have to spend time mopping up and patching up after playtimes and lunchtimes. Children fall and hurt themselves, or they fall out, fight with each other, steal money, sweets, cards or toys, spoil games... the list is endless. Headteachers, in particular, can spend an incredible amount of time dealing with playground-related issues.

Lunchtime supervisors

The emphasis for the supervisor may be on safety and related issues; concern about what the children are doing rates well below this. One group of pupils may be allowed to carry on dominating the playground, because 'at least this keeps them quiet'.

Playtime as a positive educational experience

The tragic murder of an Asian pupil in a Manchester secondary school playground opened the whole area of playground dynamics to public inspection. Race and gender provide important power dimensions, and the school will perpetuate the attitudes prevalent in society as a whole if it does nothing to promote its sense of community in the playground. If PSE is to mean anything, playtime has to be developed as a positive educational experience.

Playground strategies

In order to get a clearer idea about the causes of playtime problems in any individual school, it may help to undertake a course of structured observation and documentation of the playground at different times. How this is done will depend on the age of the children, as the outdoor play of nursery children is structured very differently from that of older primary pupils. A checklist like the one opposite can help with the documentation of children's playground activities.

Playtime checklist

1. Draw a rough map of the playground, noting:
   (i) areas that cannot be seen easily;
   (ii) markings on surfaces;
   (iii) specific provision for activities – e.g. netball posts, skipping ropes, footballs.

2. Note:
   (i) the number of pupils;
   (ii) the number of staff on duty;
   (iii) the weather;
   (iv) the time of day.

3. Older children can help with the observations, which can take several forms.
   (i) Follow or track one child during playtime, marking her or his path on the playground map.
   (ii) Jot down the activities going on in different areas of the playground, and the sex of the participants.
   (iii) Note what staff are doing.

4. Organise a pupil questionnaire like the one below. It can be either oral or written.
   (i) What do you like about playtime?
   (ii) What don't you like about playtime?
   (iii) Who do you play with at playtime?
   (iv) What causes trouble at playtime?
   (v) Is there bullying in the playground?

The following strategies may help to ensure a safer and more enjoyable playtime for all pupils.
• Adopt a whole-school policy towards good behaviour and discipline, both inside and outside the school (see pages 148 to 149 for an example of such a policy).
• Teach the children some co-operative games.
• Try changing the physical layout of the playground so that it becomes a structured playspace in which children can make choices from a range of activities. This avoids the domination of space by one group and activity, the lack of any clear boundaries between activities, and a possible lack of activities for children to choose from.

Using playground space
Carol Ross and Amanda Ryan's *Can I stay in today Miss?* (see Resources, page 156) provides a wealth of ideas for creating zones in playgrounds. Schools suffering from a high level of vandalism have particular problems, as anything movable is likely to do exactly that. However,

playground markings can be used for a number of activities:

- set games such as hopscotch;
- zones of activities, e.g. skipping, small balls, small toys etc;
- informal games, e.g. chasing;
- wall markings for target games.

The above suggestions all came, within five minutes, from a class of eight-year-olds. Children themselves will provide the ideas. Games and rules need to be developed alongside physical changes to the playground, since many children do not know how to play even very simple outdoor games such as hopscotch.

Changes can also be brought about through classroom work with pupils. This can be aimed directly at the playground, making the playground a topic in itself. The book *Can I stay in today Miss?*, mentioned above, also provides many ideas for classroom and playground use.

Alternatively, classroom work on the playground can take place as part of a more general topic. For example, the pupils who made the suggestions about playground markings were working through a topic on feelings, which was extended to include what it felt like to be the brunt of nasty comments in the playground, how children could deal with this for themselves, and how they could help other children.

SCHOOL ORGANISATION

Another way in which hidden messages are passed to children at school is through the school organisation. This can show in microcosm the way that society is divided – by age, gender, race, class and special needs. It can also show the economic aspects of gender.

There are two groups of employed personnel within schools, the teaching staff and the non-teaching staff. The teaching staff of a primary school will include the headteacher, deputy head, class teachers and assistant teachers. The non-teaching staff may include a secretary, caretaker, cleaners, kitchen staff, dinner supervisors, welfare assistants and perhaps some non-teaching auxiliaries. In some schools, fully trained nursery nurses (NNEBs) may be employed, whose position within the hierarchy as either teaching or non-teaching personnel will largely depend on their role as perceived by the headteacher. At one time, all these would have been employed by the same body, usually the LEA. Local financial management (LMS) has brought about changes which are important for the employee, but which have little bearing on how the primary child sees staff within a school.

Teaching staff

There are several issues involved in the structure of the educational hierarchy which have, or could have, important implications for gender in primary schools. Firstly, it is necessary to examine the existing structure of the primary teaching force for evidence of gender differentiation within the hierarchy. Secondly, if there is evidence of gender differentiation, it would be useful to look for data suggesting possible reasons for this. Finally, the possible implications of gender differentiation in primary schools need to be examined.

Distribution of jobs

The chart below shows the distribution of full-time primary and nursery teachers in England and Wales in 1985 by salary scale. (Source: DES).

Grade	Men	Women
Headteachers	31.5%	7.4%
Deputy heads	20.0%	8.5%
Scale 4	0.3%	0.1%
Scale 3	12.1%	7.5%
Scale 2	26.8%	41.5%
Scale 1	9.1%	34.9%
Total number	37,587	133,691

The distribution of women and men teachers in primary and nursery schools as outlined above shows that 76 per cent of women and 36 per cent of men were employed on Scales 1 and 2. Far fewer men than women enter primary teaching, yet 32 per cent of men were headteachers compared with 7 per cent of women.

When men are class teachers, there is evidence that they tend to be put with older children. A questionnaire sent out from Manchester LEA in the mid-1980s revealed that as children move up the age range, the chance that they will be taught by a male teacher increases progressively, with male teachers forming 9 per cent of the total at Junior One (Year 3) and 44 per cent at Junior Four (Year 6).

Reports indicate that nearly all part-time teachers are women and, as part-timers, they have low status and poor promotion prospects.

Prospects for promotion

The teaching unions have been responsible for several surveys at local and national level to examine the rationale for these figures. They have looked at the career pattern, attitude and professional experience of women teachers and have been unable to find any substantial reason for the absence of women in senior management positions in primary schools. The NUT survey in 1980, *Promotion and the Woman Teacher*, found that on average women teachers took seven years off teaching when they had children, and it was suggested that this 'baby break' might be at the stage in their careers when men of the same age were gaining promotion. They noted, as a related factor, that women who did gain promotion were younger and without children. Since 1980, there have been several localised surveys which indicate that the promotion prospects for women teachers are not improving and, in some LEAs, may be getting worse.

Hidden criteria for promotion to senior management posts are frequently outside the law, and the Equal Opportunities Commission has built up a series of case law decisions on specific aspects of employment such as shortlisting, interviewing and appointment. Unfortunately most of the courses run in this area are aimed at women themselves, rather than the employing bodies. This means that their effects are limited, but at least they provide an indication that the problems are recognised.

Implications

Children themselves will reveal the implications of this matter. If their school is one in which men are in positions of responsibility, they will tell you quite clearly who is important in school. Many children go through the whole of their school career without meeting a woman in a senior managerial position. The fact that men in primary schools also tend to be with older children can give them additional status in the eyes of pupils and parents.

It is also sad that many children never have the experience of being taught by a male teacher in the early years of their schooling. This is particularly poignant for children whose experience of men at home is limited, or whose feelings toward men are hostile. Both boys and girls suffer, as do male teachers, who may have a particularly limited experience of primary aged pupils.

Non-teaching staff

Non-teaching personnel make up the majority of those employed in schools. They are the caretakers, cleaners, supervisors, welfare assistants, kitchen staff etc. The majority of these are women, whose pay and status is low. Children's attitudes to non-teaching staff can be dismissive, and it is possible that the power of being male is used by some boys to treat many of these staff as inferiors – because they are women.

Senior educational administrators

The control of educational policy and decision making is largely held by men as chief officers, educational advisers, administrators and educational policy makers. National figures are available from the Education Authorities' Directory and Annual.

It is difficult to tell exactly what implications this has for policy making and organisation. An indirect effect has been that senior administrative posts have been dominated by those who have never worked in the primary sector and whose experience is inevitably second-hand.

The composition of the working parties initially set up to look at the National Curriculum also reflected this lack of primary expertise, with the result that many of the original decisions about the application of the National Curriculum to primary schools have had to be revised in the light of practical experience.

For pupils themselves this area is a hidden one, although its effects are far-reaching. Those who work within the education sector are well aware of the lessons provided by staffing matters, and the effect of a lack of role models for women and men who want to make a career in educational administration.

PSE STRATEGIES

There are various strategies that schools can adopt in order to help ensure that the issues involved in PSE are given the fullest possible coverage. Some possible ideas are listed in the next few pages.

A school policy for good behaviour and discipline

The following example is an extract from the policy statement of the Little Ealing First School and Nursery, where the policy-making is ongoing and subject to discussion. The document is a detailed one, covering the topics of classroom organisation and management, classroom interaction, the curriculum, playtimes and the playground, behaviour and discipline outside the classroom, and assemblies. The excerpt quoted below gives an idea of the sort of areas it is possible to cover in a behaviour and discipline policy.

Aims

To encourage a trusting and caring environment.
To ensure each child in the school is equally valued by all irrespective of class, race, gender, disability.
To develop good relationships in the school.
To share the responsibility for discipline and good behaviour throughout the school.
To create the best physical conditions possible around the school.
To develop an awareness which leads to proper understanding of the need to respect other people and their property.
To develop and adopt codes of good behaviour and discipline relevant to the different areas of the school.
To establish clear routines and procedures which are followed by children, staff and parents.
To foster collaborative and/or co-operative work in, between and across year groups.
To be constantly aware of the range of levels and ability in the school and the need to match tasks accordingly.
To build on children's interests, abilities and experience, involving them where appropriate.
To deal with unacceptable behaviour in a reasonable, firm and consistent manner.
To positively reinforce good behaviour regularly.

Classroom interaction

Ensure each child feels s/he has a valuable contribution to make to the classroom via:

i)　displayed work or items brought in from home;

ii)　opportunity to talk in class/group/individual discussion;

iii)　responsibility, e.g. putting things away, watering plants etc.;

iv)　a smile or touch to show you noticed her/him;

v)　positive remarks to the child her/himself, to peers about the child, to staff about the child, to parents or minder about the child.

Regularly mix children in their groups to encourage interaction of different kinds:

i)　girls and boys

ii)　all girls

iii)　all boys

iv)　varied ethnic backgrounds

v)　same ethnic backgrounds

vi)　with support staff

vii)　with High School students

viii)　with Middle School students

ix)　with parents and other helpers

Acknowledge staff members' and children's different strengths and weaknesses, enabling children to see and understand the need to share.

Work with other staff so that children and staff can witness the advantages of co-operative, team or support teaching/learning, e.g. music, story sessions, joint assemblies.

Create situations which capitalise on achievements that are not necessarily academic, e.g. music – percussion or singing, CDT – making a model, cooking, PE – skipping well.

Value children's ideas and opinions by showing them you can base topic work/sessions on their particular interests.

Work with the children to establish a code of practice in terms of behaviour, respect, responsibility and discipline.

Using picture books

There are many picture books which can be used to help children to learn about equality and respect for others. The use of such books should not be limited to very young children, as a really good picture book can be enjoyed at many different levels. Their use with older junior children can provide a way of looking at the structure of the story, and can also be a stimulus for poor readers, who might otherwise reject 'babies' books'. All the books mentioned below have been used in infant and junior schools; several could be used with nursery children.

Planet of the Monsters by Stephen May

In this book, four children – Nitya, Lee, Serena and Joe – take off in a space ship. They land on a planet of monsters, where it might be expected that they would be frightened, but the children get out of the ship and make friends with the strange-looking beings. Nitya, a girl, is the bravest.

In a Year 5 class, this theme was developed into a topic, which covered foundation subjects such as environmental studies and technology, and cross-curricular dimensions such as race, gender and special needs. The web below shows the class teacher's initial planning. It forms just one element of the teacher's curriculum plan, as it is not this school's policy that one topic should cover every area of the curriculum.

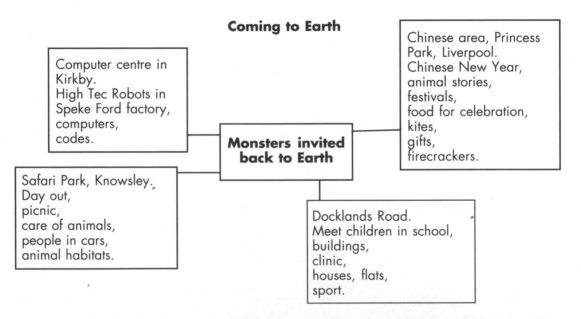

Coming to Earth

Computer centre in Kirkby.
High Tec Robots in Speke Ford factory, computers, codes.

Chinese area, Princess Park, Liverpool.
Chinese New Year, animal stories, festivals, food for celebration, kites, gifts, firecrackers.

Monsters invited back to Earth

Safari Park, Knowsley.
Day out, picnic, care of animals, people in cars, animal habitats.

Docklands Road.
Meet children in school, buildings, clinic, houses, flats, sport.

A middle infant class used the same book in a different way. The teacher told her class that she was going to read them a story about monsters, and asked the children to tell her about monsters. This they did in great detail, and some initial drama work was started with children pretending to be monsters. The story was then read and the children were asked about whether their expectations had been fulfilled. Control by a skilful class teacher meant that this discussion could be followed by work on how we should not judge people by their appearances and by our assumptions about how they will behave before we even know them.

This prediction exercise is a similar strategy to that suggested in Chapter Three, where work with Munsch's *The Paper Bag Princess* was described (see pages 65 and 66).

Long Neck and Thunder Foot by Helen Piers

This very simple story explores the feelings of two dinosaurs who meet unexpectedly. Before meeting, each dinosaur was blissfully happy in its part of the forest, believing that it was the only dinosaur on earth. When they meet, Long Neck and Thunder Foot are immediately afraid of each other; each appears threatening, angry and dangerous.

This situation raises several issues which can be discussed by very young children, and encourages them to look at a situation from someone else's point of view.
• Why were the dinosaurs afraid of each other?
• How were they different?
• How were they similar?
• How did they feel?
• What could they have done to solve the problem?

In attempting to answer these questions, some of the key concepts within the cross-curricular theme of citizenship are explored. The illustrations in the book show that the two dinosaurs are strikingly different in appearance. This raises the question of why they are different. The children themselves may suggest that the difference lies in the fact that they belong to different families, sets and groups. The dinosaurs also differ in personality, preferences and behaviour – 'just like us'. In a neutral and fictional situation, young children are able to consider the very real attitudes of tolerance and respect. When describing how the dinosaurs felt, words like unsafe, anxious, sad, worried and nervous are introduced and explored.

Rita the Rescuer by Hilda Offen

This book provides older children with an opportunity to imagine what it is like to be very little again. Younger readers and listeners can progress to this book after reading Pat Hutchins' *Titch*. Rita, like Titch, is the smallest and youngest in her family. She is considered too young to join in games with her older brother and sister. One day, a parcel arrives for her. Inside is a rescuer's outfit, which makes her look a bit like Superwoman. In this outfit she is able to perform great acts of strength and bravery. She chases away bullies, rescues her brother and sister, fixes cars and prevents accidents. Like other superheroes and heroines, she keeps her activities secret. This book works on many different levels. Some children can identify with the feelings of isolation that Rita faces at the beginning of the book. Others just enjoy her adventures as part of their own fantasies. No child has ever said that it seems odd that the story should be about a girl, although several teachers on in-service courses have recognised that this is still fairly unusual!

Juanita Havill's *Jamaica Tag-Along* also goes well with this book. This story examines the problems of being small and left out. When Berto comes along and tries to join in Jamaica's game she decides not to exclude him. This provides a shining example to her older brother, who has just excluded her.

But Martin by June Counsel

A project carried out by a multicultural advisory team in one northern authority used this book to explore very gently the differences and similarities between children. In this story, four very different children meet Martin on their way to school. Martin is even more different; he is a green Martian. A workpack was produced which provided a series of activities for teachers to work on with their classes. The importance of building up children's self-esteem was seen as an essential part of this exercise, and several of the activities were aimed at doing that.

Using books to illustrate different points of view

There are several fiction books which can be used to show children how people have different points of view. This exercise can be seen in National Curriculum terms as part of a PSE programme, but it can also be incorporated into a theme on citizenship and used to illuminate Attainment Target 2 in history, on interpretations of history. Understanding other people's points of view is an essential part of developing an awareness of the race, gender and special needs dimensions of one's life. Many familiar stories can be retold from the viewpoints of different characters; for example, 'Goldilocks and the Three Bears' could be told from Baby Bear's point of view. *The True Story of the Three Little Pigs, by A. Wolf* (J. Scieska) plays upon this idea, and both junior and infant children can enjoy it. The book provides the wolf's interpretation of events, which he claims were all caused by the fact that he wanted a cup of sugar and had a bad cold, which caused him to sneeze.

Jeanne Willis' *Dr. Xargle's Book of Earthlets* provides a funny alien's view of earth babies, and can be enjoyed at many different levels. Judy Blume's *The Pain and the Great One* looks at different interpretations of events. In the first half of the book, an elder sister records events from her point of view about her younger brother, the Pain. In the second half, her brother relates many of the same events from his perspective about his sister, the Great One. The chart below shows one way of using this book to discuss family relationships.

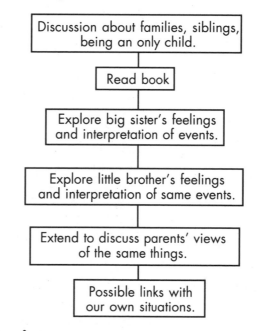

Discussion about families, siblings, being an only child.

Read book

Explore big sister's feelings and interpretation of events.

Explore little brother's feelings and interpretation of same events.

Extend to discuss parents' views of the same things.

Possible links with our own situations.

Stereotyping

This issue can be tackled very gently by asking children to look at who does what in the house. Single parents particularly cover a wide range of different jobs around the house, and younger children can talk about this, while older children can examine who does what and why. This works best when children can examine the tasks which are done for them around the house. Often, girls and boys take for granted much that is done for them. This sort of discussion also has the advantage of helping children to understand that living together is a co-operative exercise to which everyone, even the youngest in the family, contributes.

1. Who does what?

Task	Who does it?
Cleaning	
Washing-up	
Cooking	
Painting	
Bed making	
Gardening	
Fixing things that go wrong	
Making clothes	
Homework	
Shopping	

2. Jobs outside

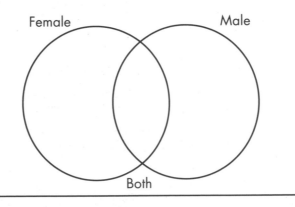

RESOURCES

Suppliers

Development Education Centres (DECs)

There is a growing network of these centres, which stock educational resources for sale or loan, offer advice to local people involved in education and provide a useful network of contacts. Some DECs undertake in-service training work. The National Association of Development Centres (NADEC) can put you in touch with your local DEC. NADEC can be contacted at 6 Endsleigh Street, London WC1H ODX.

Development Education Centre, Selly Oak Colleges, Bristol Road, Birmingham, B29 6LE.
Several publications from this centre provide an excellent starting point for teachers interested in different aspects of PSE. They are particularly strong on anti-sexist and anti-racist issues.
• *Behind the scenes* – photos and in-service activities for exploring the hidden curriculum.
• *Hidden messages?* – activities for exploring bias.
• *Theme work* – approaches for teaching with a global dimension.
• *Working now* – photographs and activities for exploring gender roles in the primary classroom.
• *Get the Picture! Developing Visual Literacy in the Infant Classroom.*
• *What is a Family?*– photopack.
• *"Where it really matters..."* developing anti-racist education in predominantly white primary schools.

LEAs

Several LEAs have produced practical guidelines for primary teachers. These are often difficult to track down unless you work for the authority concerned. The following represent a few of the more widely distributed publications.
• **Brent:** *Steps to Equality: The Report of the Primary Gender Equality Working Party.*
• **Hampshire:** *Beyond the Frame: A pack of photographs and activities.*
• **Leeds:** *Equal Opportunities: Guidelines for Primary Schools.*
• **Newham:** *Confronting Gender Bias: A Resource Book.*

Books on assemblies

Barratt, S. (1987) *The Tinderbox Assembly Book* (A & C Black).
Brandling, R. (1985) *All for Assembly*, (Cambridge University Press).
Dargue, W. (1984) *Assembly Stories from Around the World* (Oxford University Press).
Profitt, R. (1983) *Assembly Book* (Longman).
Vause, D. (1985) *The Infant Assembly Book* (Macdonald).
Vause, D. and Beaumont, L. (1989) *The Junior Assembly Book* (RMEP).
Wood, A. (1990) *Faith Stories for Today* (BBC/Longman).

Books on playground issues

Ross, C. and Ryan, A. (1990) *Can I stay in today Miss? Improving the School Playground* (Trentham Books).
Tattum, D. and Lane, D.W. *Bullying in Schools* (Trentham Books).
Grunsell, A. (1989) *Bullying* (Franklin Watts).

Books on school organisation

Acker, S. (1989) *Teachers, Gender and Careers* (Falmer).
De Lyon, H. and Widdowson Migniuolo, F. (1989) *Women Teachers: Issues and Experiences* (Open University Press).
Equal Opportunities Commission (1985) *Equal Opportunities and the Woman Teacher* (EOC).
EOC (1988) *Equal Treatment for Men and Women* (EOC).
Labour Party (1986) *Equal Opportunities for girls and boys* (Labour Party).
National Union of Teachers (1980) *Promotion and the Woman Teacher* (NUT).

Fiction for use with children

The following list gives some examples of books which have been used successfully with primary children. Several of the authors mentioned here have written other books which are just as good. Those books which are considered suitable only for the junior age range are marked with an asterisk.

Positive girl/women images

Ahlberg, A. and Wright, J. (1986) *Mrs Plug the Plumber* (Puffin).
Butterworth, N. (1989) *My Mum is fantastic* (Sainsbury/ Walker Books).
Browne, A. (1986) *Piggybook* (Magnet).
Bjork, C. and Anderson, L. (1987) *Linnea in Monet's Garden* (R & S Books).
Cole, B. (1983) *The Trouble with Mum* (Picture Lions).
Craft, R. (1988) *Fancy Nancy* (Young Lions).
*Elliott, M. (1986) *The Willow Street Kids* (Piccolo).
Fine, A. (1989) *Bill's New Frock* (Methuen/Mammoth).
Furchgott, T. and Dawson, L. (1977) *Phoebe and the Hot Water Bottles* (Picture Lions).
Gillham, B. (1988) *My Mum's a window cleaner* (Methuen).
Havill, J. (1990) *Jamaica Tag-Along* (Heinemann).
Hill, D. (1986) *How Jennifer (and Speckle) Saved the Earth* (Banana Books, Heinemann).

Hoffman, M. (1987) *Specially Sarah* (Magnet).
Impey, R. (1985) *Who's a Clever Girl, then?* (Heinemann).
*Kaye, G. (1987) *A Breath of Fresh Air* (Andre Deutsch).
McKee, D. (1987) *Snow Woman* (Andersen Press).
Mahy, M. (1987) *The man whose mother was a pirate* (Picture Puffins).
Mooney, B. (1987) *I don't want to!* (Magnet).
*Naidoo, B (1988) *Journey to Jo'burg* (Young Lions).
Offen, H. (1985) *Rita the Rescuer* (Magnet).
Still, K. (1987) *The Tractor Princess* (Orchard Books).
Storr, C. (1967) *Clever Polly and the Stupid Wolf* (Puffin).
*Taylor, M. (1980) *Roll of Thunder hear my cry* (Puffin).
Williams, J. (1986) *The Practical Princess and other Liberating Fairy Tales* (Hippo).

Positive boy/man images

Armitage, R. and D. (1990) *When Dad did the Washing* (Andre Deutsch).
Bradman, T. and Browne, E (1986) *Through My Window* (Methuen).
Browne, A. (1986) *Willy the Wimp* (Magnet).
De Paola, T. (1983) *Oliver Button is a sissy* (Magnet).
Endersby, F. (1986) *Man's Work* (Child's Play).
Galloway, P. (1985) *Jennifer has two daddies* (Women's Press).
Graham, B. (1987) *Crusher is Coming* (Collins).
Greenfield, E. (1989) *Grandpa's Face* (Hutchinson).
Hughes, S. (1978) *Helpers* (Armada).
Mahy, M. (1987) *Jam* (Magnet).
Ormerod, J. (1984) *Moonlight* (Picture Puffins).
Schoop, J. (1986) *Boys Don't Knit* (Women's Press).
Zolotow, C. (1988) *William's Doll* (Harper and Row).

Positive images with a special needs dimension

Ahlbom, J. (1987) *Jonathan of Gull Mountain* (R & S).
Althea (1983) *I use a wheelchair* (Dinosaur Publications).
Anderson, R. and McNicholas, S. (1988) *Jessy Runs Away* (A & C Black).

*Doherty, B. (1989) *Spellhorn* (Hamish Hamilton).
*Exley, H. (1981) *What it's like to be me: written and illustrated by disabled children* (Exley).
Griffiths, V. (1987) *My class visits the nature centre* (Franklin Watts).
Zelonky, J. *I Can't Always Hear You* (Blackwell).

Different points of view

Ahlberg, A. and J. (1986) *The Jolly Postman* (Heinemann).
Blume, J. (1988) *The Pain and the Great One* (Piper).
Cole, T. (1979) *Fourteen Rats and a Ratcatcher* (Picture Puffin). (Excellent on different points of view, but poor on gender stereotyping.)
Piers, H. (1984) *Long Neck and Thunder Foot* (Picture Puffin).
Scieska, J. (1984) *The True Story of the Three Little Pigs, by A. Wolf* (Viking Kestrel).
Willis, J. (1990) *Dr. Xargle's Book of Earthlets: An alien's view of earth babies* (Red Fox Picture Books).

General books

Askew, S. and Ross, C. (1988) *Boys Don't Cry* (Open University Press).
Brown, C., Barnfield, J. and Stone, M. (1990) *Spanner in the Works: Education for racial equality and social justice in white schools* (Trentham Books).
Carrington, B.and Troyna, B. (eds) (1988) *Children and Controversial Issues: Strategies for the Early and Middle Years of Schooling* (Falmer).
Dixon, B. (1990) *Playing them false – a study of children's toys, games and puzzles* (Trentham Books).
Fisher, S. and Hicks, D. (1985) *World Studies 8-13* (Oliver & Boyd).
Galloway, F. (1989) *Personal & Social Education in the Primary School* (Pergamon Educational Productions).
ILEA (1986) *Primary Matters: Some Approaches to Equal Opportunities in Primary Schools* (Harcourt Brace Jovanovich).
Lang, P. (ed) (1988) *Thinking About ... Personal & Social Education in the Primary School* (Blackwell).
Miller, B. and T. (1990) *That's Not Fair: A resource for exploring moral issues in primary and middle schools* (Wheaton).
National Union of Teachers (1989) *Towards equality for girls and boys: guidelines on countering sexism in schools* (NUT).
Reay, D. (1990) 'Girls' Groups as a Component of Anti-

sexist Practice – one primary school's experience' in *Gender and Education*, Vol. 2, No. 1.

Rogers, C. (1985) *Freedom to learn* (Merrill).

Weiner, G. (1985) *Just a Bunch of Girls* (Open University Press).

Whyld, J., Pickersgill, D. and Jackson, D. (1990) *Anti-sexist Work with Boys and Young Men* (Whyld Publishing Co-op, Moorland House, Caistor, Lincs LN7 6SF).

The Woodcraft Folk *Getting on with others: A resource pack for 6-9 year olds; Images: A resource pack for 9-13 year olds* (The Woodcraft Folk, 13 Ritherdon Road, London SW17 8QE)

8 MANAGING EQUAL OPPORTUNITIES

So far this book has examined gender issues in regard to both the formal and the informal curriculum, looking at the ways individual teachers and schools can monitor what is going on in the classroom, and suggesting strategies to strengthen good practice.

This chapter will look at two other issues that are important in ensuring that equal opportunities permeate the whole curriculum:
• the gender implications involved in testing and assessment;
• the role of the equal opportunities co-ordinator.

GENDER IMPLICATIONS FOR TESTING AND ASSESSMENT

One of the major issues raised by the introduction of the National Curriculum is that of testing and assessment. Assessment is an essential part of the National Curriculum (NCC, *From Policy to Practice*). The Education Reform Act requires pupils to be assessed formally at or near the end of each key stage, which means ages seven and eleven for primary pupils. The requirement for schools to publish their aggregated results for pupils at Key Stage 2 (i.e. age eleven) is seen as one way of opening up communications between schools and the wider community. It is also likely that public pressure will force all schools to publish the results of their seven-year-olds.

Since the abolition of the 11-plus in most areas, primary schools have largely escaped this very visible display of the product of their endeavours. As described in Chapter 3, the final results of the 11-plus were frequently gender-related and indeed gender-corrected.

Publication of results has an important bearing on the role of any co-ordinator as the government, through the NCC, requires schools to monitor the performance of constituent groups such as boys and girls and members of ethnic minorities.

The acknowledgement that gender issues may have some bearing on assessment and testing is one of the reasons why the Equal Opportunities Commission submitted evidence to the Task Group on Assessment and Testing (TGAT). This evidence was published in full as Appendix F in the TGAT report.

The importance for primary schools of gender issues in relation to assessment and testing can be seen in four major areas:

- access to curriculum and relevance of curriculum content;
- testing;
- teacher assessment;
- monitoring and reporting.

Access to curriculum and relevance of curriculum content

Access

Throughout this book, questions have been raised about whether pupils have equal access to the school curriculum. If some pupils are denied full access, they are unlikely to perform as well as they could, either in the programmes of study or in the standard assessment tasks (SATs).

It has been shown that the problem of access to the curriculum is complicated, and that it starts at a very early age. When children first start school or nursery, they can be given a wide choice of activities. If this choice is completely unstructured, it can result in some children choosing the same narrow range of activities every day. A more structured approach can avoid this, by extending and developing experiences rather than reinforcing existing narrow choices. For older classes, access to the curriculum can be limited if some children claim a disproportionate amount of the teacher's time and resources.

Examples of limited access are seen in activity-based mathematics and science work, where some children may be able to gain more practical experience than others. Limited access may also affect assessment in language work, where boys can dominate mixed groups, but gain less practice in listening and responding to what others say.

Relevance

Primary teachers work hard to ensure that programmes of study are made as relevant as possible for all pupils. There is an almost universal acknowledgement that children learn best when they can find relevance and interest in what is presented. Evidence has shown that relevance has gender-related variables, both in what teachers choose to present and in what they perceive as being of relevance to children. Once teachers are aware of this, it should inform their curriculum planning. So, too, should the need to ensure that particular children's interests do not have priority over others because some pupils are more successful at attention-seeking.

As with structured play in the nursery, it is important that children's interests are broadened to include areas with which they are less experienced. Child-centred education should not result in a curriculum based on a number of potentially very narrow areas of interest derived from children's leisure activities.

The obligation to provide a broad and relevant curriculum is an essential part of curriculum planning. Assessment and testing of children is likely to reflect the children's own understanding of the way in which programmes of study have been presented to them.

TESTING

Testing is one of the most controversial issues raised by the Education Reform Act. This is possibly because so many older primary teachers have memories of taking the 11-plus themselves. Their anxieties are two-fold. Firstly, there is a recognition that the 11-plus distorted the curriculum for many 10- and 11-year-olds, because of the extreme importance given to the examination in some schools. I remember very clearly doing test papers week after week when I was in primary school, until the final great day when we sat the 11-plus. This fear of curriculum distortion will only be resolved, one way or another, when the SATs have been in operation for several years.

Bias

The second anxiety about testing primary pupils comes from the belief that testing can be a source of bias, denying opportunities to some pupils. The early belief that the 11-plus would equalise opportunities was tempered in time by the recognition that testing and examinations might be biased in favour of one particular gender, social or ethnic group. The failure of some social groups to attain grammar school places was seen as a failure of the tripartite system of education set up under the 1944 Education Act. The IQ-testing element of the 11-plus was discredited as a way of assessing a child's educational potential. This experience has no doubt influenced the reactions of many teachers to the idea of any form of national testing at seven and eleven.

There are two forms of bias addressed by test developers.

Item content bias

Today, good test constructors are well aware of the need to avoid sexual and racial stereotypes. However, it is difficult for tests used over the whole country to be completely unbiased in terms of content. For example, inner city children will relate to some experiences, practical exercises and pictures better than rural children, and vice versa. There will also be a difference in the relevance of test items to boys and girls, whether they come from the same cultural groups or different ones.

Statistical item bias

This occurs where items or questions in tests favour one or other group disproportionately.

Caroline Gipps of the University of London Institute of Education, speaking on gender issues in assessment at an Education Network Seminar held by the Equal Opportunities Commission (EOC), provided the following as an example of statistical item bias: 'car is to tyre as (tank) is to caterpillar' was disproportionately easy for boys in one test while 'dough is to pizza as (pastry) is to pie' was disproportionately easy for girls.

Other, more specific gender issues have arisen in relation to testing pupils, and these were reported to TGAT in the EOC submission. For example, girls do particularly well on verbal reasoning tests; boys do well on multiple choice questions. The EOC report voiced concern about the established differences in test performance between girls and boys throughout the age range from seven to sixteen and across the curriculum. They pointed out that to standardise test scores according to different gender norms would constitute unlawful discrimination.

One reason why testing has become a matter of such concern is that schools are now required to make themselves as economically viable as possible. Local Management of Schools (LMS) ensures that published test results will be seen as a key indicator of a school's performance. If at primary level it is found that girls or boys perform better overall, this means that schools with a disproportionate number of boys or girls may have test results which reflect this gender imbalance.

A system of national testing from seven to fourteen is likely to have a strong effect on children's lives. The gender implications are complex, and they have importance for teaching as well as testing. An equal opportunities co-ordinator needs to monitor this so that the issues can be raised and addressed in advance of published results.

TEACHER ASSESSMENT

This has been described as the 'most potentially dangerous area in national assessment' (Caroline Gipps, 1989). There is a vast amount of evidence to show that teachers' judgements of children are deeply affected by stereotypes. Evidence from the secondary sector indicates that girls and boys doing equally well in mathematics tests were differentially allocated to O Level or CSE because girls were seen by their teachers as 'not really bright' and working to their full potential while boys were regarded as 'really bright' but 'underachieving'! (The Royal Society, *Girls and Mathematics*.)

Similar findings have been made in the primary sector. An assessment of the educational potential of individual children may be elusive, but it is nevertheless important for primary teachers. Formalising criteria for teacher assessment has important gender implications. The nursery chart shown here indicates how one school has attempted to incorporate equal opportunities issues into its assessment procedures. The chart, from Prescot C.P. School, forms just one section of a nursery 'record of achievements' folder. Like other school charts in this book it is an ongoing document, subject to discussions among all those concerned.

Social and Emotional Development

Monitoring and reporting

Monitoring the performance of constituent groups, such as boys and girls, and members of ethnic minorities, is seen as an important part of the development of assessment techniques and record-keeping policies (NCC 1989). In *An Introduction to the National Curriculum* the NCC, acknowledging help from SEAC, state under the heading 'Equal Opportunities for All' that:

'all pupils have their own educational needs and some have needs which require the provision of additional resources or opportunities, including those who are gifted as well as those with particular learning difficulties'.

The document suggests that:

'examination of the curriculum experience and profile shape of individuals within any constituent group (such as boys and girls, or members of particular ethnic groups), will make it possible to detect any significant differences in their attainment relative to the teaching or age group as a whole. This information will provide a basis for developing classroom and school policies to promote equality of opportunity'.

THE ROLE OF THE EQUAL OPPORTUNITIES CO-ORDINATOR

Some primary schools now give responsibility for equal opportunities co-ordination to a member of staff. The terminology describing the post may vary; some co-ordinators are known as postholders, some as facilitators, and others as curriculum leaders. Schools which have highly formalised management teams may wish to include equal opportunities as a senior management responsibility. In other schools, however, the subject may be given less priority.

In many cases equal opportunities is taken on in addition to several other areas of responsibility. It may be given to a particular individual for a variety of reasons, such as:

• personal interest and expertise on the part of a particular member of staff;
• awareness that the area needs to be given priority;
• a response to advice from outside the school, i.e. from the LEA.

Frequently, equal opportunities is linked with responsibility for other National Curriculum dimensions, such as race and special needs.

Job specification

As with other curriculum posts, there are certain duties expected from the postholder. These may be written down as part of the individual's job specification, or the postholder may have to develop his or her own specification.

Responsibility for National Curriculum dimensions such as equal opportunities presents particular challenges. Circular Number 6 and Curriculum Guidance 3 make it clear that equal opportunities should permeate the whole curriculum. This means that the co-ordinator for equal opportunities has an extremely far-reaching brief.

Jim Campbell, in his book *Developing the Primary School Curriculum*, provides an excellent guide for co-ordinators who have no written specification, even though he is writing about subject co-ordination rather than the more nebulous area of cross-curricular dimensions. His classification of the role of a postholder makes a useful starting point for those holding the responsibility without written guidelines.

He suggests that postholders need curriculum and interpersonal skills in order to carry out their responsibilities. He then subdivides these into five key areas:

Curriculum skills cover skills and qualities involved in knowledge about the particular curriculum area for which the postholder has responsibility:

1. Knowledge of subjects – the postholder needs to keep up to date and must know the conceptual structure and methodology involved.

2. Professional skills – the postholder must be able to draw up a programme of work, implement and maintain it and assess its effectiveness.

3. Professional judgement – the postholder must know about various materials and approaches in her or his subject and discriminate between them, relate them to children's developmental stages, manage the school's resources, and achieve a match between the curriculum and the pupils' abilities.

NB Campbell was writing before the National Curriculum. Today's co-ordinators could usefully add

'Development within the National Curriculum framework' to the three curriculum skills suggested.

Interpersonal skills are skills and qualities that arise from the postholder's relationships with colleagues and other adults:

1. Social skills – the postholder must be able to work with colleagues, leading discussion groups, teaching alongside colleagues and helping to develop their confidence, advising probationers etc.

2. External representation – the postholder must represent his or her subject to outsiders (other teachers, advisers, governors, parents etc.).

The skills briefly outlined above can be expanded as follows.

Knowledge of subjects

There is a growing amount of data about how an awareness of equal opportunities informs good practice. The idea that gender issues have a basis in knowledge can surprise some primary practitioners. Yet this awareness is essential if co-ordinators of the curriculum areas are to monitor and evaluate the accessibility and relevance of their field for all pupils. The bibliography at the end of this chapter lists several books which can provide a good knowledge base for any primary co-ordinator.

Professional skills

Some equal opportunities co-ordinators are required to draw up policy statements. Chapter 2 provides an outline for these and points out the importance of ensuring that the final statement is the result of consultation. A policy statement is virtually worthless unless attainable targets are set. As with other curriculum areas, constant monitoring and updating are needed to ensure progress. As fellow subject co-ordinators learn more about equal opportunities, this task becomes very much easier because, when subject guidelines are updated, implications for equal opportunities become an automatic criterion.

Professional judgement

More and more material is available for use with primary children which directly or indirectly involves equal opportunities issues. As with any other area of the curriculum, professional judgement is needed in deciding on the criteria for selection. The field is still a relatively new one in the UK and there is still available some worthy but potentially unsuitable material, whose use with children may reinforce sex stereotyping.

Formal checklists provide a simple means of identifying essential attributes to look for when selecting materials. Any checklist should incorporate equal opportunities criteria so that new purchases can reflect school policies. If staff have worked out the criteria together, this process can develop wider perspectives on the issues involved. One of the best resources for looking at bias and insensitivity in materials is *Everyone Counts*, produced by ILEA for primary mathematics. A useful in-service activity is to look at this publication's criteria for ways in which materials may be biased or insensitive. This is best done after staff have had a chance to draw up their own criteria.

A further advantage of spending time discussing criteria for resource selection is that it can help to persuade colleagues of the need to sort existing materials. Otherwise, it is a daunting prospect for any one member of staff to be given the overall responsibility for sorting.

The table below shows the ILEA's criteria for assessing mathematics materials.

Are certain groups of people ignored or diminished?
  invisibility – are they there at all?
  tokenism – are they there but just for show?
  status – are they there but in low-status roles?

Is a wide range of lifestyles presented?

Is the use of stereotypes avoided?

Are there offensive visual images?

Are people's religious, cultural and moral values acknowledged and treated sensitively?

Is a Eurocentric view of the development of mathematics presented?

Are individual children's feelings and experiences treated sensitively?

Is the language used predominantly masculine?

Are the interests of girls and boys provided for equally?

Do the materials use childhood myths which are irrelevant to many children?'

Development within the National Curriculum framework

When the first National Curriculum document was published out, there was a tendency to try to relate everything that was being done in schools at that moment to particular attainment targets and programmes of study. Since then wider-ranging support material has been published by the NCC and SEAC, which illustrates very clearly the experimental nature of much of their earlier documentation. The initial consultative document, produced in 1987, failed to mention several areas of educational experience. Later documentation redressed this imbalance.

The role of the co-ordinator is to ensure that colleagues are familiar with the relevant documentation, and can apply it to the policy guidelines and practices of their own particular specialist areas.

It may also be necessary for the equal opportunities co-ordinator to show how gender issues relate to such cross-curricular themes as citizenship, economic and industrial understanding, and careers education and guidance.

Social skills

For teachers working in primary schools, gender and race issues are notoriously sensitive, since they touch upon individuals' personal lives. The distinction between personal and professional roles is very clear cut for some teachers, while others see their professional and personal lives as part of a continuum. Gender issues tend to blur any clear-cut distinction, and there is a very real danger that professional viewpoints can be interpreted as personal attacks. Women who have taken long career breaks may feel threatened by those who carry on working while also involved in childcare. Those who have taken the decision to carry on with their work while raising a young family can be made to feel guilty because they have adopted a different approach to childcare. Men whose wives are at home looking after them and their children may feel threatened by equal opportunities issues which question this traditional role for women. Unmarried men and women may get annoyed because their views are ignored or discounted.

The equal opportunities co-ordinator is also likely to be stereotyped – as anything from a 'trendy' who has jumped on the latest bandwagon, to the middle-class, bra-burning 'women's libber' who hates men. Summing up an individual in terms of a stereotype makes it easy for colleagues to ignore their ideas and dismiss their suggestions out of hand. It is worth remembering that those who feel threatened by new ideas are often the most vociferous in discussion, and that they tend to react in a similar way to other issues, not just equal opportunities.

Men who have taken on the role of equal opportunities co-ordinator have particular problems because support networks tend to be made up mainly of women, and the men's particular difficulties are rarely recognised. It is worth remembering that the fact that men make up a small proportion of primary class teachers means that this sort of situation is found in many other areas of co-ordination apart from equal opportunities.

One of the social skills required by the co-ordinator is to show respect for the opinions of others, while retaining a clear view of what does constitute good equal opportunities practice.

Steve Harrison and Ken Theaker, in their valuable handbook *Curriculum Leadership and Co-ordination in the Primary School*, have a whole section on methods of resolving conflict. They point out that conflict can be a positive force, and that one of the skills needed by any curriculum leader is the ability to recognise this potential, so that conflict is not avoided but controlled.

They also make the important point that the 'Munich' method of resolving conflict rarely results in any effective change. This method is characterised by a naïve belief that 'niceness' will prevail, so that 'crunch' issues are not raised and discussed.

The vagueness of some equal opportunities policy statements is a good testimony to the long-term ineffectiveness of the Munich method.

External representation

As with most curriculum co-ordination, a great deal depends on the existing relationships between the school and its various constituent bodies. It is essential that gender, race and special needs dimensions are seen as fundamental to good practice by all those who form the wider school community. There is little point in having a visionary equal opportunities policy statement which is limited to the schooling elements of children's lives.

The existing mechanisms for informing parents and the wider school community about what goes on in schools have been heavily criticised over the past few years. The idea that there was a 'secret garden of education' has been under attack since the start of the 'Great Debate' in the mid 1970s. Since then, informal practices used to draw in the local community have been formalised, and have frequently been set out in a written statement of procedures.

'The whole school community' is a vague description of the differing groups who have an interest in the school. A school is, after all, more than just a building; it is living beings who give it its identity. Most of the book has concentrated on gender issues in relation to the direct consumers of education – the children and their teachers. However, they come from a wider community, which also has a vested interest in what goes on within its school. Other interested people include:
• parents and carers of pupils;
• employees of the school and LEA who work at the school – welfare assistants, nursery nurses, caretakers etc;
• school governors;
• LEA support personnel – advisory teachers, school nurses, school doctors etc;
• community support services, such as the police liaison officer;
• local councillors;
• local secondary schools;
• employers;
• religious bodies linked formally or informally to the school.

Parents and carers of pupils build up a view of their child's school from a variety of different sources, including their memories of their own schooling. Prior to a child's admission, most parents will visit the school to see and speak with the headteacher. In this preliminary discussion, many of the expectations of both sides are aired informally. The school prospectus may state the school's aims more explicitly, and the final decision of a parent to enter a child for a particular school marks an acceptance by both school and parent that they have similar aims for the child. If equality and social justice is seen by the school as a key aim, this should form part of a policy statement which parents should see before their child enters the school. A school discipline policy is worthless if parents are unaware of its existence or unwilling to support the school in upholding the policy.

A child's carers, inside and outside school, need to have an agreed policy on what constitutes acceptable and unacceptable behaviour. Parents and teachers need to understand each other's systems of rewards and sanctions. Problems occur later if these very basic issues are not discussed early on.

The question of future expectations is also important here. Parental expectations can be discussed and the school's hopes for its pupils can be seen in a positive light.

The introduction of policy statements after children have been admitted creates a different challenge, which schools have tackled in various ways. Open days and evenings are frequently used to inform parents and carers of changes in school practice. Information about the equal opportunities issues which permeate the curriculum can be provided in this way as part of the ongoing process of reporting to those interested in how the school is working.

Parents who come into school regularly to help, and employees of the LEA and community support services, need to understand the underlying principles of a school's equal opportunities policy statement. Racist and sexist comments and stereotyped forms of behaviour that are unacceptable from children should not be tolerated from adults who are helping out in school. Regular visitors to the school should be able to see the permeation of good equal opportunities practices.

It is also important that a variety of people are involved in the life of the school; men and women, black and white, old and young, able-bodied and those with special needs. The community outside is a mixed one, and this needs to be reflected inside the school. Too often 'parental' support means, in practice, 'mothers'.

Governors also need to be kept informed of new developments. The EOC have produced a booklet for them,

Equal Opportunities and the School Governor, and the Labour Party has produced its own guide for governors entitled *Equal Opportunities for Boys and Girls*. Governors need to be aware of the legal implications for them of the Sex Discrimination Act, and they should also be informed of ways in which they can help schools 'increase the equality of opportunity between the sexes in schools for both pupils and teaching staff' (EOC 1985). Changes in the case law mean that this information has to be constantly updated. Many LEAs and church organisations provide governor training, of which equal opportunities is frequently a component.

Most secondary schools are only too familiar with the inhibiting effects of traditional choices of subjects and careers, and there is growing awareness of the importance of primary education in widening children's horizons before they become too fixed. Some schools have used gender issues as part of primary-secondary liaison, with teachers from both sectors working on projects which extend primary children's experiences.

Employers have a vested interest in the education of a flexible work force. Many of the large trade unions, such as the Transport and General Workers Union, have equal opportunities units. These are not only committed to recruitment of more women into the unions, but also realise that changes in the gender composition of the work force will have far-reaching effects for their members.

Some of these unions have educational units, and their regional educational officers can be useful initial contacts for primary teachers. At the moment, most of the unions' initiatives in schools are focused on raising secondary pupils' awareness of industry. But at a local level, these same contacts can be used in primary schools, providing useful links for teachers wanting to contact men and women engaged in non-stereotyped jobs. Some unions have special women's officers, who may also be interested in this particular educational area. They will also probably be prepared to talk to the children about their own working experiences.

Religious bodies have varying degrees of commitment to social justice, which may or may not include equal opportunities. Some churches have provided recommendations on equal opportunities policy-making which acknowledge the relevance of gender issues in the search for social justice.

The relationship between any school and the community it serves is, now more than ever, a key element in its eventual survival. Equality of opportunity is simply part of good educational practice, which recognises that learners are of equal value and have unlimited potential for development. Education has a vital role to play in redressing the inequalities and injustices which exist in society. Schools do make a difference and primary schools are the foundation for every child's formal learning programme.

RESOURCES

Curriculum co-ordination

Alexander, R. (1984) *Primary Teaching* (Holt).
Campbell, R.J. (1985) *Developing the Primary School Curriculum* (Holt).
Harrison, S. and Theaker, K. (1989) *Curriculum Leadership and Co-ordination in the Primary School: A Handbook for Teachers* (Guild House Press).
McFarlane, C. and Sinclair, S. (1986) *A sense of school - an active learning approach to inservice* (available from Development Education Centre, Gillett Centre, Selly Oak Colleges, Bristol Road, Birmingham).
Mosley, F. (1985) *Everyone Counts* (ILEA – now distributed by Harcourt Brace Jovanovich).

Government publications

DES (1989) *From Policy to Practice* (DES).
Equal Opportunities Commission (1985) *Equal Opportunities and the School Governor* (EOC).
Equal Opportunities Commission (1988) *Local Authority Equal Opportunities Policies: Report of a survey by the Equal Opportunities Commission* (EOC).
EOC (1989) *Equal Opportunities: the implications of the Education Reform Act: Report of Education Network Seminar* (EOC).
National Curriculum Council (1980) *The National Curriculum and Whole Curriculum Planning: Preliminary Guidance* (Circular No. 6, NCC).
NCC (1989) *An Introduction to the National Curriculum* (NCC).
NCC (1990) *Economic and Industrial Understanding* (Curriculum Guidance No. 4, NCC).
NCC (1990) *Citizenship* (Curriculum Guidance No. 5, NCC).

Task Group on Assessment and Testing: *Report*, 1988 (TGAT).

TGAT (1988) *Task Group on Assessment and Testing: A digest for schools* (DES).

General

Antonouris, G. and Wilson, G. *Equal Opportunities in Schools: New Dimensions in Topic Work* (Cassell).

Boyd, J. (1989) *Equality Issues in Primary Schools* (Paul Chapman).

Browne, N. and France, P. (1986) *Untying the Apron Strings* (Open University Press).

King, R. (1978) *All Things Bright and Beautiful: A Sociological Study of Junior Middle Schools* (Falmer).

Labour Party (1986) *Equal Opportunities for Girls and Boys: What every Labour governor needs to know* (Labour Party).

National Joint Council for Local Authorities' Administrative, Professional, Technical and Clerical Services (1988) *Equal Opportunities Joint Advisory Booklet* (NJC for APT & C).

New Internationalist (1990) *Reaching for Certainty: Fundamentalism* (August).

Skelton, C. (1989) *Whatever Happens to Little Women? Gender Issues and Primary Schooling* (Open University Press).

Tutchell, E. (1990) *Dolls and Dungarees: Gender Issues in the Primary School* (Open University Press).

Weiner, G. (1985) *Just a Bunch of Girls* (Open University Press).